Safety Zones

BOOKS BY THE SAME AUTHOR

Where Do I Go to Buy Happiness?
Your Troubled Children
Loneliness
Woman Beyond Roleplay
The Whole Christian
To Anger, With Love
Can I Talk to You?
You Can Be Your Own Child's Counselor
Loving Begins With Me
Coping
Beyond Loneliness
Growing Through Rejection
Contributor to the *Evangelical Dictionary of Theology*
    Walter A. Elwell, Editor

Safety Zones

Finding Refuge in Times of Turmoil

ELIZABETH SKOGLUND

WORD BOOKS
PUBLISHER
WACO, TEXAS

A DIVISION OF
WORD, INCORPORATED

SAFETY ZONES

Unless otherwise indicated, Scripture quotations are
from the
King James Version of the Bible.

Library of Congress Cataloging in Publication Data:

Skoglund, Elizabeth.
  Safety zones.

  1. Peace of mind—Religious aspects—Christianity.
2. Consolation.   I. Title.
BV4908.5.S55   1987   248.8'6   86-32518
ISBN 0–8499–0555–9
ISBN 0–8499–3078–2 (pbk)

In this book names and circumstances have been altered
to protect the privacy of the people involved.

Printed in the United States of America
7 8 9 8   BKC   9 8 7 6 5 4 3 2 1

This book is about *Safety Zones*. The ultimate safety zone is God. Yet because He knows our needs, He has also provided each of us with many lesser, day-to-day safety zones.

The writing of this book occurred at the end of several personal tragedies which enabled me to see more clearly than ever the value of my own safety zones and intensified my desire to share the concept of safety zones with others. I hope that reading what follows will help you find yours.

For those people in my family who were a special childhood safety zone for me and who are now a part of that great cloud of witnesses of Hebrews 12:

My parents, *Ragnar Emanuel Skoglund*
and *Elizabeth Alvera Benson Skoglund,*
who were my earliest safety zone
and who introduced me to the One
who was to become my only permanent safety zone

My aunt, *Lydia Alfreda Benson,*
who was there at the end
as it turned into the beginning

My aunt, *Ruth Caroline Benson,*
to whom I was always special

My uncle, *David Alfred Benson,*
who knew how to comfort a small child

My aunt, *Esther Benson Jones,*
and my uncle, *Blanton Withers Jones,*
who filled my childhood with so much joy.

And for the *Emil Karl Erselius* family, who as friends and next-door neighbors completed my unique childhood safety zone of family and friends, and who today continue to provide a valued safety zone of friendship.

Acknowledgments

The author wishes to express her apreciation to Christian Literature Crusade, Inc., for permission to use copyrighted material from the Amy Carmichael books, *Rose from Briar, Gold by Moonlight,* and *Candles in the Dark.* Poems used by permission of Christian Literature Crusade, Ft. Washington, Pa. 19034.

Contents

Chapter One

Safety Zones

I like to rape women," the man said with studied calmness as he sat across from me in my counseling office. "Really?" I replied, my voice attempting to equal his in calm detachment.

It was a Saturday afternoon. The man was a new referral, a professional in his field of architecture. When he came into my office I had felt a sudden visceral fear of the kind that arises out of pure instinct. I had sensed danger, and then admonished myself not to be so silly. Silly, that is, until he opened his mouth and started telling me about himself, his past violence against women, and his official criminal record.

For a brief, horrible moment I felt like a trapped animal confronted by a savage beast, without a way of escape. Because it was Saturday afternoon, I was the only person still working in what suddenly seemed to me to be a truly huge medical building. (Actually it has only two floors!) I had opted to do without clerical assistance on this particular day, and even the telephone was beyond my reach. Besides, the telephone, which had always felt like a form of protection, now seemed ridiculously unimportant. After all, I reasoned, if this man attacked me he was hardly going to stand by and wait for me to make a phone call!

I felt trapped, alone and vulnerable. I had no zone of safety, no place to which I could retreat. For a few endless moments, I experienced a terrifying feeling of having no way out. Even though I came through unharmed, for a long time afterwards just the memory of the incident was enough to bring back on a visceral level that terrible feeling of no place to hide.

As I recently watched the movie, *The Hiding Place*, for the second time, I was impressed with the similarity between one scene in that movie and my own feelings of vulnerability on that Saturday afternoon in my office. The Ten Boom family's sole survivor, Corrie, had just watched her sister, Betsy, die in the middle of the horror of Hitler's infamous death camp, Ravensbruck. In her despair and all alone, she rushed out from the barracks where her dead sister lay and ran blindly through the bleak snowdrifts. As that small, gaunt figure ran in the blackness of the night between the monotonous rows of gray barracks, the scene epitomized what it is, even for one brief moment, to have no place of comfort, no safety zone.

Some forty years later, in January 1986, many of us experienced somewhat different and yet related feelings of disbelief, horror, and helplessness as we watched firsthand the explosion of the space shuttle, *Challenger*, with its fiery billows of smoke spiraling out over the ocean. The idea of such a tragedy unfolding in front of the eyes of the entire world, including those well-versed in space technology, without anyone being able to do anything to stop it was mind-boggling! Here we sat, in utter impotence, watching human beings die in a spectacular burst of fire. There was stunned disbelief—and, again, no escape, no place to run—for them or for us as we watched.

Even if they are usually on a less extraordinary level, each of us human beings has moments of acute helplessness where there seem to be no available supports left. A first day at school or a new job can produce such feelings. The experience of standing by the new grave of a loved one or knowing for the first time that one's child is on drugs can also bring with it the feeling of needing to run but finding no place to go.

More everyday occurrences, too, like a recalcitrant child, a sleepless night, or a busted water heater can produce feelings of being overwhelmed. Too much to do and no one who understands can make the strongest person among us feel the need for some extra resource to which he can turn for solace, some kind of safety zone to which he can go for refuge and refreshment.

A safety zone is a place, a thing, a concept, or a person into which we can retreat, find safety, and become refreshed. These safety zones usually remain constant in our lives for at least a time, and they enable us to go on. They range in type from the simple to the complex, the mundane to the sublime. A familiar face in a new town, a hot bath after a long day, a quiet piece of music after the noise of a big city, clean sheets, hot chocolate, the smell of roses or night-blooming jasmine: these are simple safety zones that we use and never think about. Yet we would miss these sources of refreshment if they were to disappear.

Simple safety zones are often taken for granted; we hardly notice them. We are perhaps more aware of the sublime, and yet even with these we tend to overlook their value: the timeless inspiration of a hymn, the confidence of friends who have proven their loyalty through the years, faith in God, the inspiration of a great piece of art or music. Whatever the safety zone may be at any given time, it provides a place of relief and refurbishment. We run to it for safety and emerge from it better equipped for what we must do.

The concept of safety zones is not a new one, nor is it limited to us human beings. It seems instinctive to all forms of life. When I go to my favorite retreat by the ocean, I sometimes love to sit by a tidepool and just watch the various forms of life. Usually there is a sea urchin somewhere in the vicinity. If I take a piece of driftwood and ever so gently poke at this creature, it will invariably pull back into itself. It just sort of folds up. Its safety zone from the threat of danger is to retreat.

My dog, Thackeray, does much the same thing. He is terrified of the noise of firecrackers or cap guns, for example, and when he hears these noises he will race to my side and hide his nose under my hand until he can hardly breathe. Faulty as his thinking may be, Thackeray feels safe as long as his nose is hidden! That is his safety zone.

The behavior of children is often strikingly illustrative of human feelings and behavior in general. Even small infants seek safety from the strange new world into which they have entered. The safety zones which they find are relatively simple, like the comfort of being held or the warmth of a bottle.

But if the example of small children is striking in its simplicity with regards to safety zones, it is even more striking in its portrayal of the harshness of having no safety zones.

Not long ago, I watched a newborn baby withdrawing from cocaine addiction. The infant just lay there, shaking and whimpering, with a look of agony on his face. There was no comfort possible. There was no safety zone, for this child was far beyond the point of deriving much comfort from warm milk or loving arms. I felt as I watched this child that perhaps he epitomized that stark, helpless feeling which comes to all of us when life deals us a particularly heavy blow and we find ourselves, for the moment at least, with no place to run, no available refuge.

As children grow beyond the helplessness of infancy and as the pressures of everyday life begin to impinge upon their existence, they start a more active search for safety zones which opens up endless possibilities. Tents, caves, ditches, secret boxes where they can hide their treasures: these all become important to the growing child as safety zones into which he or she can retreat when life becomes stressful. They represent a retreat from adult demands and threats, as well as providing a symbolic sense of privacy and self-identity. As the child grows into adulthood, the need for safety zones does not diminish, but the search becomes more self-conscious, and at times we are embarrassed by our vulnerability.

A while back I heard a story about a woman who was alone on a business trip in a large city in the United States. The day before she was due home, she went shopping. Among other things, she bought a soft teddy bear for her youngest child. That evening her husband telephoned her in her hotel room to tell her that her father had died suddenly of a heart attack. The news was completely unexpected.

Alone in a strange city, the foundations of this woman's life had suddenly crashed. Feeling as though she was without a friend in the world, she slowly unwrapped the teddy bear. As she held it close and fell asleep that night, she felt a little foolish. Here she was, thirty-five years old, sleeping with a child's toy. Yet, because the emotional pain was so great, she didn't care how it might look. She simply accepted the only comfort she had at hand until she could return to the greater comfort of her family and home. Because her more usual safety zones were not readily available, she accepted a safety zone which had often comforted her in childhood.

At its most primitive level, a safety zone offers what it says: safety. When my mother was a little girl growing up on a farm in Wisconsin, she would often cut through a neighbor's pasture on her way home from school. Then one day someone put a huge, fierce bull in that pasture. My mother barely outran the bull and scrambled under the fence to safety with the bull at her heels. The other side of that fence was literally her safety zone.

We have all experienced, many times over, a sense of relief in the pit of our stomach when we literally reach a place of safety after being in great physical danger. It happens everyday in the form of near-misses on the road. Nor does the safety zone need to be a physical one. Every time a student passes an important examination in school or a busy mother with three small children finds a time of quiet into which she can retreat, each of them has found and used a safety zone.

Safety zones provide more than just safety, however. They can be used to comfort and to refurbish us for future work, when without them life with all its fast change and just plain heartache might well annihilate us. They help us go on.

One of my most cherished letters is one I received jointly from my friends Joseph and Judith Fabry after I had published a book on loneliness and then, within a month, had lost almost all my family as a result of a car accident. In part they wrote:

> We were sorry to see that life has found it necessary to test you so severely, but I know from your writing that you will take up this challenge and grow stronger and [become] a better therapist from it. . . . You are not alone. It makes your book on loneliness stand there and urge you one step further, onward, in company of those who share and understand suffering. . . . The process of surviving and overcoming all the pain and shock is slow, a long one. . . . The darkness does not remain. After a while there is again light and healing strength.

Such a letter and such understanding became one of many safety zones which both comforted and refurbished me at that time of loss and change. It challenged me to go on.

In his own book, *The Pursuit of Meaning*, Dr. Fabry describes his early life in Austria prior to World War II, his studies as a law student at the University of Vienna, and then the cataclysmic changes which occurred in his life as a Jewish person in Europe after Hitler took over. In the midst of much personal disillusionment involving the loss of his career in law and even including the loss of home and country, he also endured the death of his father, who died in a cattle wagon on the way to a concentration camp, and later his mother, who had been with his father. When he finally came to the United States, he had indeed lost most of his safety zones. In his words:

I arrived in New York a penniless refugee, jobless at the tail end of the depression, an ex-attorney with the knowledge of laws no longer existing even in my own country, a writer without a language. I met a woman who did not care what I had (or did not have) and who perceived what I was—what I could become if only someone believed in me. She did not tell me this; she acted upon it by marrying me.[1]

In this woman Joseph Fabry found a major safety zone at a time when the loss of earlier safety zones had been great. He found safety, comfort, and a way to go on.

Usually we lose our safety zones one at a time rather than from one cataclysmic blow. A relative dies, a job is lost, we move to another part of the country—each in its time. If we are wise, we try to space the timing of those changes over which we have control. Then there will be a period of time to adjust to each change before another occurs. There will be time to build safety zones.

But sometimes the changes come unbidden, several at a time. Thus it is wise to have a number of safety zones so that even when multiple losses occur they do not devastate us. It was interesting to me to learn that Columbus never let any of his ships sail without five anchors. He did not want to take the chance of finding himself anchorless in a turbulent, uncharted sea.

Many times we have no choice over the timing of our loss of safety zones. Still, when a safety zone is lost, recovery is necessary if we are to remain whole.

Sometimes only time is required in order to get used to the change—for example, to adjust to the fact that the new job has different demands than the old one. But, especially if our supply of safety zones is small or if we have lost several important safety zones at one time, we may need to develop new safety zones before we can recover. While we are doing that, for a time we may have to rely more heavily than usual on those safety zones which still remain.

Perhaps that is why, after a death, we humans instinctively tend to group together with family and friends to eat meals and trade memories. It probably explains why, when things are going along smoothly in my life I like to try new restaurants; but when I have just undergone some great loss or change, I tend to go to old and familiar places which make me feel that at least something in my life has remained the same.

During times of great change or loss, counseling can sometimes become a temporary safety zone—a bridge, so to speak, over the turbulent waters. Psychologist Rollo May eloquently describes the safety zone of counseling:

> It draws the other human being for a moment out of the loneliness of his individual existence and welcomes him into community with another soul. It is like inviting the traveler in from his snowy and chilly journey to warm himself for an hour before the fire on another's hearth. Such understanding, it is not too much to say, is the most objective form of love. That is why there is always a tendency on the part of the counselee to feel some love toward the counselor, this person "who understands me." There are few gifts that one person can give to another in this world as rich as understanding.[2]

Nor, in the healing of emotions when a person has been torn apart by change and loss, is the cure restricted to only the human aspects of counseling. It is not the counseling relationship alone which becomes our safety zone. Continues Dr. May:

> Finally, after all our discussion, we come to the realization that there is a great area in the transformation of personality which we do not understand, and which we can attribute only to the mysterious creativity of life. . . . As the motto has it, "The physician furnishes the conditions— God works the cure." Like the doctor, we may bind up the wound; but there are all the forces of life welling up in their incalculable spontaneity in the growing together of skin and nerve tissues and the reflowing of blood to perform the healing. Before the creative forces of life, the

true counselor stands humbly. And his humility is not of the false sort, for the deeper his understanding of personality the more clearly he realizes how minute his efforts in comparison to the greatness of the whole. He says with the psalmist, "Lord, this is too wonderful for me." I am myself frank to say that when the limits of my own understanding are reached, I understand the miracle of the transformation of personality in terms of that age-old but ever new concept, the grace of God.[3]

For it is during difficult times that we often draw close to God and experience His comfort in ways we would never know during those times when life is level and change is minimal. God becomes, more than ever, a safety zone.

Since I was about fifteen, Amy Carmichael's writings have been greatly used in my life during times of stress. Her books in general have reminded me that God is my greatest safety zone, and the words of the following poem in particular have often challenged me to find meaning in the seeming chaos around me:

> Before the winds that blow do cease,
>   Teach me to dwell within Thy calm;
> Before the pain has passed in peace,
>   Give me, my God, to sing a psalm.
> Let me not lose the chance to prove
>   The fullness of enabling love.
> O Love of God, do this for me:
>   Maintain a constant victory.
>
> Before I leave the desert land
>   For meadows of immortal flowers,
> Lead me where streams at Thy command
>   Flow by the borders of the hours,
> That when the thirsty come, I may
>   Show them the fountains in the way.
> O love of God, do this for me:
>   Maintain a constant victory.[4]

Safety zones promote health. They stabilize us during times of stress, and they enable us to go on after the most terrible of life's blows. The paradox of the resiliency and yet the fragility of human beings has never ceased to amaze me. At times we crumble at even the hint of rejection in someone's voice, while at other times we endure great tragedies and seem to become stronger through the experience. Whether or not we have and make use of our safety zones can often make the difference between growing through an experience or being destroyed by it.

It is important, however, to realize that safety zones are only temporary buffers which enable us to recover and go on. They are never meant to be permanent places of residence. The dinner after the funeral may soften the blow of the death, but a permanent, nightly funeral dinner would become ghoulish and destructive. Friends can be supports throughout our lives, but ultimately we must each live our own lives and make our own decisions, or again the safety zone becomes corrupted into something negative.

Even God, who is the only safety zone we have which never fails and does not change, commanded Joshua in the Old Testament to get up off his knees and act. For, says God, "Get thee up; wherefore liest thou thus upon thy face? Israel hath sinned . . ." (Josh. 7:10–11). These words are in marked contrast to but in perfect balance with Samuel's statement of "God forbid that I should sin against the Lord in ceasing to pray for you" (1 Sam. 12:23). The safety zone of prayer is always there, and that in itself is comforting. But it is meant to be a place from which we then go out again into the world.

This year as I once again looked forward to celebrating Christmas Eve, I paused to reflect. All the preparations for the traditional Swedish smorgasbord were completed except for the final serving of the dishes, which ranged from pickled herring and potato sausage to the Christmas cookies, cut into their various festive shapes and sprinkled with colored sugar.

Red candles were lighted all over the house, and in its usual place in the dining room stood my little tree with its colored lights which my father bought me when I was four. And again this year, as in every past year, my favorite thing was the big tree in the living room. The toy ornaments, the old colored balls from the past, the tin ornaments from a memorable time in Mexico: all these gave me that warm feeling which is a result of a pleasant blending of the past and the present. But most of all there were the lights: small twinkling lights, icicle lights, colorful bubble lights and, this year, a new addition: running lights which created the illusion of small white lights literally running all over the tree.

The night seemed so comfortingly familiar. Memories from childhood flooded my mind: waiting for the aunts and uncles to arrive; knowing that I would always go to bed in new pajamas that night; eating the special foods which had been prepared for days before; and, the highlight of the evening, opening gifts. When I was a child, Christmas Eve was a magic night of dreams come true. Then, after all the festivities of the Swedish Christmas were over, in true American style I, like children all across this country, would fall asleep hoping to catch a faint sound of reindeer landing on our roof.

Even on the Christmas that fell a week after my father was buried, the small, modestly decorated tree and the evening of modified smorgasbord and small gifts shared with family and friends provided the comfort of the familiar and reminded all of us of the true meaning of Christmas. The realization of the miracle of Christmas, God become Man, increased my awareness that my father had joined that great cloud of witnesses in Heaven. His last words on this earth which were known to us were, "It is the grace of God which has brought me this far, and it is the grace of God which will bring me through." Those words in themselves were a comfort.

Actually, that year, when the poinsettia plants reminded

me more of funeral decorations than of the celebration of Christmas, the meaning of Christmas as a time of rejoicing in God's greatest gift to mankind became more real to me than ever. Christmas once again became a safety zone which this time in particular brought comfort.

It is forty years since those first childhood Christmases in California after my family moved here from Chicago. It is forty years later, and yet it seems like yesterday; for the Swedish tradition of celebrating Christmas on Christmas Eve, Americanized in many ways both for convenience and preference, has remained with me. It provides a point of stability in my life each year. It carries with it memories of Christmas past which cannot be taken from me. It has become ever-expanding in its potential for change within the basic structure which remains for Christmas present. It is one of the safety zones in my life.

Chapter Two

Beyond Survival

When we were growing up, most of us had a place, a "hangout," where we gathered with our friends. For me, that place was a local coffee shop which exists to this day. Invariably we kids always ordered the same thing: cherry coke and french fries with lots of salt. In that day, no one had talked to us of the dangers of salt; so, undaunted by lessons of modern nutrition, we poured away from the salt shakers. It was over such a snack that I made such momentous decisions as not to play a lead part in the senior play, even if the teacher did think I was a natural for it. (Since the part called for a crabby, old-maid school teacher, I spent some added time wondering how much of a compliment it was for the teacher to have called me a "natural" for the part!)

The coffee shop was our place, our safety zone, where we could talk and think and let down in the middle of the rigors of growing up. Once we got married or started jobs or finished college and began our careers, most of us forgot that cherry cokes even existed.

Then a few years ago I lost, for all practical purposes (except for an elderly aunt who survived), my remaining family in a car accident. I have a few relatives in places far removed from where I live, but for one reason or another I have never really known them well. And so my elderly Aunt Lydia, who survived that accident, became increasingly precious to me—both for herself and for what she represented as a link with the past.

With help, my aunt lived at home until just short of her

ninetieth birthday, when she became very ill and was hospitalized. The evening of her death was a night which was to become etched into my memory forever. As I stood by her bed she told me she was dying, and I knew her assessment was accurate. All my instincts to fight for her life came to the forefront, so after speaking some faltering words of comfort I left the room to talk to the nurse.

It was at that moment that I was confronted with one of the toughest questions of my life from a doctor and a nurse who really didn't want to ask it: "If she stops breathing, do you want us to do the heroics—machines, heart massage, and so on—or do you want us just to use medication and make her comfortable?"

It was a question I had thought of in the abstract for several years, and in recent months it had been a major topic of concern with patients in my counseling office. But now it was MY question for MY family, and I suddenly had no answers. I knew I had to go someplace and think. I needed a safety zone from the terrible stress. My usual place, the beach, was too far away, for I sensed that I had little time left.

Then suddenly, without much thought, I found myself heading for that old coffee shop with an insatiable desire for a cherry coke. This time I had outgrown my need for the heavily salted french fries, and I could now afford a large cherry coke instead of a small one. But otherwise everything was the same as many years ago, and the sameness felt comforting. In this place, which was old and familiar to me, I could think and pray. Children screamed across the aisle, and the restaurant was bustling with this year's crop of teenagers. But I barely heard them. For a few minutes I was safe; I could think; I had my zone of safety.

We human beings have always used safety zones to get through the stresses of life. At times that safety zone is a favorite book; sometimes it is a place, such as a restaurant or the beach; often it is a belief in God or a close relationship with a friend. The potential variety of safety zones is as great as the numbers of people who inhabit this earth, and most of us have a number of them.

Many times, however, we do not recognize these safety zones as such, and therefore we often fail to make full use of them. Then, too, at times we lose a safety zone, and it needs to be replaced for use in future times of change and stress. For safety zones are anchors; they provide refuge; they help us to recover and regroup from the stresses of life. They enable us to go beyond mere coping or survival.

As a means in helping us to go on, one of the most important functions of a safety zone is to help us pause and gain perspective. I have what I call my "back to earth days." When the demands of life become too overwhelming, I take a day at home to putter. Sometimes I do something like rearrange the objects on my coffee table, or change furniture around, or copy recipes from magazines. At other times I watch an old movie or read a book I haven't had time to get to. But more frequently than not, I bake bread.

There is something about baking bread that brings me back to earth from all the stresses of everyday modern life. Maybe it's kneading the dough, in all its simplicity and physicalness, that helps the most in relaxing me. Maybe it's the time required to let the bread rise that forces me temporarily to slow down. But whatever it is, these "back to earth days" and baking bread in general have become for me a safety zone where I can take some time and gain a perspective on what I'm doing. It is as though my feet get firmly placed again on earth, and the problems of yesterday begin to look solvable. Afterwards, that which looked hopeless no longer seems so impossible, and that which seemed complex appears less so in the light of a new day.

As I think these thoughts, my mind begins to drift back to a very old history lesson and I remember the mathematician Archimedes and his famous statement: "Give me a place to stand and I will move the earth." A more modern translation might read, "Give me the refuge of a safety zone, and I, too, will move at least my part of the earth."

In the sense that they provide a perspective, safety zones are the antithesis to high-wire living and what is so commonly referred to today as burnout. For no one sees life with any sense of perspective from a state of mental and physical exhaustion. One of the best ways I know to combat modern burnout is to stand back from my situation and, with the use of some particular safety zone that works for me, regain my perspective.

Sometimes all that may be required is a brief conversation with a valued friend or a walk with my dog. At such times, temporary distancing from my task is my greatest requirement. If physical fatigue is a factor, I may just need a short nap. But at other times, more prolonged physical rest and retreating to my favorite ocean spot may be what I must have before I can recover and go on with any kind of effectiveness. Such time is not wasted time; it is indeed the very factor which will minimize waste in our lives. Rest in itself can be a safety zone, a way to gain perspective and go on.

I was deeply struck with this thought as I was reading a book, *The Wounded Healer,* based on the letters of Bible translator J. B. Phillips. The book talks of the emotional pain which Phillips endured for the better part of his life, and it rightly emphasizes his courage in ministering to people as he did in spite of what at times amounted to deep emotional torture. At one point in the book, Phillips describes his emotional state by quoting Michael Hollings:

> I can with difficulty endure the days but I frankly dread the nights. The second part of almost every night of my life is shot through with such mental pain, fear and horror that I frequently have to wake myself up in order to restore some sort of balance. If I don't manage to do that it quite often takes me three or four hours after waking to recover anything like a normal attitude towards life.[1]

The book describes the pressure of Phillips's lifestyle in the following way:

Even under control, his was a massive programme of writing, speaking, conferences, broadcasts, visits to cities and towns in America and throughout Great Britain. From 1955 to 1961 he maintained this killing program and at last, when he was fifty-five, he cracked. As one doctor put it, he was "scooped out."[2]

To me, the saddest lines in the entire book are those written by Phillips to a physician: "I have an invincible feeling, that IF I could rest even for a few days nature would very quickly restore me to my normal health and spirits."[3] Those are sad lines to me because they seem so true and so untried. One can only speculate that perhaps J. B. Phillips's own prescription might have been his best cure if tried consistently throughout his life.

I have come to believe that the old "burn out for God" slogan which I heard so frequently from the pulpit as I was growing up is damaging and unscriptural. To the contrary, the Bible speaks of our bodies as temples of the Holy Spirit and therefore as not belonging ultimately to us. It would seem to follow that these temples are to be kept up and taken care of. To this end, the development and use of safety zones in preserving physical as well as psychological and spiritual well-being are vital.

Even Christ had his safety zones when He was on this earth. When He felt the necessity, He left the crowds, with all their burning needs, and sought a place of solitude and rest. He did this even though He as God-Man knew each of their individual needs in accurate detail. In Gethsemane He leaned heavily on His disciples. They were an anchor for Him, unreliable as that anchor became at times. On this earth He was often weary, but it does not seem that burnout was the principle of His life. He stopped, He rested, He enjoyed friendships, and He spoke often with

His Heavenly Father. He developed and used His safety zones.

Speaking with greater clarity to me than anyone else I have read of the dangers of overdoing, and of its lack of productiveness as well, Grattan Guinness wrote to his daughter, Geraldine Taylor, daughter-in-law and biographer of Hudson Taylor who founded the China Inland Mission:

> How well I understand that nervous breaking down from which you have suffered. Let it be a warning. There is a limit you should not attempt to pass in exhausting labors. It is not easy to fix it, but experience shows pretty clearly where it is. I have gone beyond it at times, when all the foundations of life seemed gone. I cannot express what that means, and hope that you will never know. Most people have no conception how thin the foundations are which keep them above the abyss, where the interests of life exist no more. Learn to say "No" to invitations or calls to labour which destroy the power to labour and the possibility of service.[4]

For Geraldine, safety zones, involving routine and regular hours of sleep and daily exercise, became life-saving. And one of her greatest anchors was found in her close relationship with her physician-husband, Dr. Howard Taylor. For forty years he was with her, pulling her back from doing too much, buffering her from the often very public life which she lived. I am sure that he can take great credit for the balanced books which Geraldine wrote, books which contain deep spiritual truths as well as carefully documented records of one of the greatest missionary works ever attempted.

Geraldine Taylor was an extremely talented, productive human being who has had a profound influence on the Christian Church as well as on Christian missionary work around the world. But if she had not developed and used the safety zones which worked for her, the perspective and even the very volume of work which she produced would have been greatly diminished. In her words, she would have been in her "grave long ago."

Safety zones, however, provide us with benefits other than a sense of perspective. For it is through the use of safety zones that we can be both comforted and encouraged in the middle of all the vicissitudes of life. This, too, enables us to go on.

When I was a child, Saturday was a safety zone for me. After all the weekly challenges of growing up and learning, on Saturday morning I could sleep in. Then, somewhere around midmorning, my sister and I would be awakened from our sleep by the aroma of my mother's coffeecake baking in the oven. On that morning alone the combined scent of cinnamon and yeast became our alarm clock. To this day, even though I now work on Saturday, Saturday mornings are special to me. They are still a sort of safety zone in that they are a prelude to the end of my work week. Back then, in those childhood days, I felt the comfort of the familiar, of the predictable, of my parents' love. Now I still feel comfort from those memories.

For safety zones do not have to be elaborate to be effective. A hot bath after a tiring day, a greeting from a faithful dog, an evening of music, a favorite book, a special dinner, a chat with a friend: all these and countless others can be safety zones. What helps each of us will vary according to our own personalities and backgrounds, but often they are very simple. The aroma of my mother's coffeecake was not an earthshaking event in my childhood. I doubt that my mother thought twice about it in terms of child-raising. But it became an important childhood safety zone which will have its effect on me for the rest of my life. It probably has a lot to do with the effectiveness of my "back to earth days."

For the everyday changes and stresses of life, safety zones give us that sense of security which we need to go on. These safety zones are not dramatic; at times we scarcely

notice them, and many of us use them without even knowing that they are there. Yet, conscious or not, the use of
safety zones in our everyday living helps most of us live
more comfortably and more productively. Then, when the
major catastrophes of life hit us with their stunning, nauseating blows, it is partly through use of safety zones that we
survive at all or that we go beyond survival and grow
through the experiences.

Several years ago, on a Saturday afternoon, a single
phone call changed the course of the rest of my life. My
aunt and mother had been in a car accident which was to
take my mother's life within a few days and which would,
for all practical reasons, take all of my remaining family
except for my elderly aunt. As I stood outside of that hospital emergency room, I knew that my life would never
again be the same. And I determined in those few moments that this experience would not destroy me, but that
I would grow from it in whatever way God wished.

After the initial crisis was over, my more earthy needs of
exhaustion and emotional fatigue needed some very practical attention. Again, there were safety zones which
helped. Shortly after the funeral, after my aunt had been
properly attended to, I went to my favorite ocean hide-
away and refurbished myself for two relaxing nights. The
steadiness of the sea, the familiar old hotel, old friends,
and time away from demands all effected their cure. It was
my place, my zone of safety. Life would change again many
times, and pain and stress would never be eradicated from
my life. But for now I had my place of retreat.

Then, sometime within that same time span, I wrote in a
journal kept just for myself at that time: ". . . I am alone."
Then, remembering the line from Madeleine L'Engle, I
added, "'I will never again be anyone's child.' But I can go
on and live in my friendships and do and become those
things which were meant for my life—my writing, my patients, and above all honor God. In these ways I will deserve my parents' trust in me. I love them both and will

always miss them. But I must go on, for 'I have miles to go before I sleep. . . .'"

In this time of great crisis in my life, meaning became a primary safety zone, combined more specifically with a faith in God. I would not suffer this pain in vain. I would grow. I would honor God. I would help others. I would go beyond mere survival. I would go on. This was my safety zone of meaning.

Psychiatrist Viktor Frankl speaks of unconditional faith in unconditional meaning. To believe this is to tap into a very concrete safety zone. In his book, *The Will to Meaning*, Frankl states,

> Day by day I am confronted with people who are incurable, men who become senile, and women who remain sterile. I am besieged by their cry for an answer to the question of an ultimate meaning to suffering.
>
> I myself went through this purgatory when I found myself in a concentration camp and lost the manuscript of the first version of my first book. Later, when my own death seemed imminent, I asked myself what my life had been for. Nothing was left which would survive me. No child of my own. Not even a spiritual child such as the manuscript. But after wrestling with my despair for hours, shivering from typhus fever, I finally asked myself what sort of meaning could depend on whether or not a manuscript of mine is printed . . . But if there is meaning, it is unconditional meaning, and neither suffering nor dying can detract from it.[5]

For many years, starting long before the death of any of my family, one of my most fundamental safety zones has been that of meaning. For me as a Christian, this meaning is often indivisible from my faith in God, for He becomes the object of my unconditional faith. When nothing seems right or makes sense, I can rest in the Old Testament question, "Shall not the Judge of all the earth do right?" (Gen. 18:25). To me, that which I do not understand about

God does not disprove Him. To the contrary, His unknow-ableness is one of the greatest proofs of His existence. For if I, a finite human being, could totally know and under-stand God, He would cease to be God!

In the New Testament Paul speaks along a similiar line: "Nay but, O man, who art thou that repliest against God? Shall the thing formed say to him that formed it, Why hast thou made me thus? Hath not the potter power over the clay, of the same lump to make one vessel unto honor, and another unto dishonor?" (Rom. 9:20–21).

Again, "Shall not the Judge of all the earth do right?"

The other day I asked a Jewish friend who had been in the Nazi camps during World War II what had been her greatest safety zone—what had gotten her through. I ex-pected a complicated answer. In contrast to my expecta-tion, she replied with one word: *Prayer.* Then she told me about how, when her family was escaping from Germany to Holland, they were picked up and brought to the Gestapo. Through the whole two hours or so that built up to this, my friend had been praying. Then, as they went to the Gestapo headquarters, my friend, who at the time was still a child, turned to her father and said, "Don't worry; God will get us out." And He did.

Later, when they were all actually in the camps, the family became separated. Once again, prayer with uncon-ditional faith that God would indeed do right was my friend's safety zone. This time she became absolutely sure, as she sat alone in the camp and prayed, that somehow God would bring her family back to her from whatever camp they were in—and in time for Hanukkah! Up to the last minutes there seemed to be no reason for her faith. But by Hanukkah they were together!

The fact that in these examples the answers to my friend's prayers were positive did not in itself make God a safety zone to her. For, indeed, God could have said no rather than yes. The real safety zone was to be found in the fact that He was actually there to be prayed to and could be trusted to do all things well.

Another prisoner of war, this time a Turkish World War I prisoner whose name is unknown, wrote a poem along these lines which was published years ago in the *Sunday School Times:*

I will abide, tho night is drawing nigh;
The cloud and darkness now obscure the sky;
I know thy sorrows, see thy falling tear.
Give me thine hand, for I am ever near.

The earthly joys are fleeting fast away;
Lean upon Me, and I will be thy stay:
My grace is all sufficient, rich and free.
Have perfect faith, I will abide with thee.

Mine eye is watching o'er the troubled child;
My arms shall guide thee, though the path be wild;
'Mid storms and tempests to my bosom flee:
Have perfect faith, I will abide with thee.

A little while, and then it will be light;
Thy faith shall be exchanged for perfect sight;
No fears to vex thee, nothing to molest,
For thou shalt be with Me in perfect rest.

When friends forsake thee, I will be thy Friend;
My love shall keep thee until life shall end,
And when heaven's golden gate thine eye shall see
I will eternally abide with thee.

A safety zone? Most certainly. And in God we have a safety zone which is eternal. It will always be there for us. And yet seemingly in contrast to the permanency of God as a safety zone, safety zones as such must be used as something temporary. They are places of refuge from which we then go out again to the world around us to do the task to which God has called us. For if we try to live

37

permanently within a safety zone, we will find that they may contribute to our destruction rather than our healing or growth.

A while back, I saw a lady in my office who had once found solace in prayer. Then she started praying for longer and longer periods of time. Finally her children were neglected and her marriage disintegrated while she found herself compulsively praying during every waking hour. Her safety zone had ceased to be a safety zone. Because of deep psychological problems which had no real relationship to religion but came out in that form because she was religious, her safety zone had become a place of torment because she had decided to stay there.

When I was a child and used to play softball at school, I loved to hit the ball with the bat and then fly through the breeze to first base, second base, third base, and—best of all—home base. I rarely made it to home base in one run, however, and so I can remember the relief I felt as I made it to any base just short of being tagged and declared out. Those bases were safety zones. You were safe! No one could declare you until you ventured off the base to the next one, which in turn became another safety zone. No one ever stayed permanently on any base. They were meant as places of temporary safety. They were places to go on from.

And so in our lives our safety zones are places from which to go on. I didn't move back into the coffee shop that night of my aunt's death. I didn't even start going there every night after work. It was like first base in those childhood softball games; it gave me just enough time to catch my breath. And, in this case, it gave me the security of the past to draw upon while it provided a place where I could think and decide what to do next.

In his book, *Twentieth Century Journey,* referring to the first three quarters of the twentieth century, William Shirer comments, "That brief whiff of time, as time goes, that has comprised my own span, encompassed more changes, I believe, than the previous thousand years. It has been an interesting experience to have been born in the horse-and-buggy age and to have survived into the nuclear era."[6] I would dare to venture a guess that in the years which have passed since Shirer's comments were written down, the pace of change has accelerated to an even greater speed.

It may not be inaccurate, then, to say that we are a people facing more change and threatened change than any group of people before us on this planet Earth. How well we handle this change may be largely dependent on the use we make of our safety zones.

I do not know if it is because my Aunt Ruth was a missionary with the China Inland Mission and therefore as a child I heard many stories about that work, or if I would have been impressed by its work regardless. But I do know that of all the missionaries who have affected my life, Hudson Taylor, the founder of that great mission, influenced me the most, along with Amy Carmichael of Dohnavur in India. The major safety zone for Hudson Taylor's work for God in China could be summarized in the words, "God's work, done in God's way will never lack God's supplies."[7] To that refuge Hudson Taylor constantly retreated.

As I have been thinking about safety zones as enablers toward going on, repeatedly a simple scene from the life of Hudson Taylor has come back to me. Mr. Taylor had lost several of his children, along with his wife and close companion, Maria. He had buried them all in Chinese soil, far from the comforts of his home in England. From the British press as well as from some of his own missionaries, there had been scorching criticism of his policies in China—adopting Chinese habits and dress in order to build a church which would be Chinese, not British or American.

Years later the wisdom of this policy would be apparent to all, when foreigners were expelled from China and the indigenous church survived and flourished in spite of persecution. But of these later times Hudson Taylor knew nothing. He only knew the loss, the criticism, and loneliness of one burden after another. But repeatedly he clung to his Lord as his anchor.

Hudson Taylor's biographers, Howard and Geraldine Taylor, describe this safety zone with a poignant intimacy—a description which has remained in my memory since I first read it at the age of fifteen:

> The secret of his own strength was not far to seek. Whenever work permitted, Mr. Taylor was in the habit of turning to a little harmonium for refreshment, playing and singing many a favorite hymn, but always coming back to— "Jesus, I am resting, resting, in the joy of what Thou art; I am finding out the greatness of Thy loving heart.". . . .
>
> Frequently those who were wakeful in the little house at Chinkiang might hear, at two or three in the morning, the soft refrain of Mr. Taylor's favourite hymn. He had learned that, for him, only one life was possible—just that blessed life of resting and rejoicing in the Lord under all circumstances, inward and outward, great and small.[8]

Unconditional faith in unconditional meaning: an anchor for many through the centuries of the history of man.

Whatever our age and regardless of our status in life, all of us need safety zones if we are to survive and go beyond mere survival in this world of change. My counseling office is probably the only counseling office in the world which has a large green frog sitting in the corner. His name is Herbie, and as far as my adult patients are concerned he is just a toy box. But to the very young he is a safety zone.

Sometimes when children first come to see me, Herbie is all that reassures them. For not only is he always filled with treats to be chosen from when the child leaves, but Herbie is like a friend who never tells secrets. Several children who have been afraid to talk much to me until their second or third visits have turned to Herbie upon leaving after their first visit and said what in later visits they would say to me: "Goodbye, Herbie. It's been nice meeting you!"

Not long ago, I came out into my waiting room to find a pretty child of about eight or nine standing alone. "Are you Elizabeth?" she asked. I replied in the affirmative and asked her who she was. When she said her name, and when I then looked up to see her father now standing behind her, a myriad of memories flooded my mind of the same little girl at age three, who had come to me for counseling. I was glad to see her so grown up, so obviously happy. But I realized that to her the past was all a blur. She really didn't remember much about our sessions or even me.

Then I asked the magic question: "Do you remember Herbie?" There was an instant grin of recognition, for Herbie had been one of the safety zones of her childhood. Once again she eagerly went to get her treat from the large green frog, and as she did so she relaxed. Through Herbie she remembered more clearly this place in which she had found help at a very young age. She felt again the refuge she had found in counseling. And she remembered once more the safety zone she had found in a green frog named Herbie.

The Lord Gave, And the Lord Hath Taken Away

*W*hen computers were first introduced into the high school counseling office where I used to work, the result was total chaos. First of all, no one appeared to know much about using them, and so they never seemed to work. A favorite excuse for a late printout of student schedules was "The computer broke down" or "The computer made an error."

Actually, for the most part, human beings made errors in feeding the computer, and the computer merely printed out those errors! All the mistakes, however, gave us ample excuse to say what man has said about change since the beginning of time: "It won't work!" (Eventually, of course, it did work, no thanks to our negativism.)

"It won't work!" Why? Because it's new and untried. "Surely nothing can work better than what is old and proven," we reason. All change, "good" or "bad," threatens us to one degree or another because change is new and new is scary.

Many of us pride ourselves on our innovativeness and openness to new ways. Most of us even like the excitement of the new, as long as it is no more threatening to us than a long awaited vacation to a place we've never been before. And even then we quickly look for safety zones by getting to know the people around us and becoming physically familiar with our new surroundings before their newness overwhelms us. However, when change strikes at any major area of our lives, most of us react instinctively with anxiety.

45

A while back I bought new furniture for my office. The old furniture was so tacky I could barely give it away; I had bought it used from another therapist about thirteen years before, and it had gone well beyond its time of service. One of my more affluent patients, whom I thought would be impressed with the fact that after all I did have some measure of decorative taste, walked in and said in horror: "Oh, you got rid of your wonderful old chair!"

Now, keep in mind that this woman did not mean "wonderful" as in "beautiful," or "old" as in "antique." She meant "wonderful" as in "comfortable"—in the sense of that lumpy, well-used feeling that so often accompanies long use. She meant "old" as in "familiar." In the middle of massive personal changes in her otherwise very successful life, my office had become an important safety zone for her, and now I had dared to change it.

Actually, almost no one liked my new office; they just got used to it. Only new patients seemed to appreciate my decorative efforts, because to them my office was new anyway; and, for them, it would soon grow old and safe.

Given what seems to be an inborn resistance to change, it is no wonder that the sweeping transitions of late twentieth-century living are causing a great deal of anxiety to most of us. We live in a time of particularly widespread change. As in that high school counseling office, often our first reaction is denial and avoidance. But after that initial withdrawal, all we can do to cope with *unavoidable* change is to go with it, to some degree at least, and in the process to develop safety zones to buffer the change. Perhaps never before in all of man's history have we needed safety zones so desperately as now.

So often small children illustrate our adult needs most poignantly. I remember one little boy who was brought to see me because his natural mother was giving him up for adoption and he was overwhelmed by a rather sudden transition from her to his adoptive home. At the end of several sessions, one day he curled up safely in the corner of my office playroom and asked, "Could I just live here? Could I stay here forever?"

This playroom and the atmosphere of safety in which he was allowed to express his anger and fear had become a safety zone for that little boy. Like so many of us, he had found a safety zone and was loath to leave it. But like the rest of us, he could only use that safety zone as a temporary respite, not as a permanent dwelling place.

In the times in which we live, we sometimes feel like that little boy—scared and alone in a changing world. For there are many changes occurring around us that deeply affect our lives but about which we have no direct choice.

In times past, unavoidable change occurred, but slowly. We had time to adjust to the change, and soon it became old instead of new. My parents, for example, watched firsthand the transition of flying from the days of Charles Lindbergh and his doing of the "impossible" to the present day, when many of us fly frequently and without much thought. But that change took years; there was time to adjust. Now we are inundated by constant change, all happening faster than our ability to absorb it and much of it centering around areas which are fundamental to our well-being and even to our very existence.

Because of its fundamental importance to the quality of our lives, the institution of the family is at the top of the list of areas affected by unavoidable change. Perhaps in no other single area has the change been so complete and so destructive. In my counseling office, it is more unusual for me to see a family which is intact than it is to see a family that has been through a divorce and at least one set of new parents and stepchildren. This is not because families that stay together do not have problems; indeed, the process of keeping a family together can require people to face problems rather than run from them and to learn what it is to build a marriage and family.

However, a great many families in this country have already split up at least once. In the eyes of many, marriage is a temporary contract to be entered upon tentatively to see if it works. Or there is no marriage at all because "marriage just ruins a good relationship." Indeed, many question the value of the traditional family to our present society. Even Christians, who would probably agree with the importance of marriage and the family, are not always living up to what they say they believe. When one considers the high divorce statistics, one could certainly ask whether most marriages and families start with much basis in reality.

For their part, children have grown accustomed to changing parents from time to time and moving back and forth between parents. When I heard that the new thing in custody settlement was to give the children the family home, with the parents moving in and out on alternate months, I felt we had reached an all-time low in the disintegration of the American family. When one considers the trauma of children or parents moving back and forth from home to home, it becomes obvious why people in this position would be in desperate need of some kind of safety zone, something safe and familiar with which to buffer the stress of changes over which many of them may have little choice.

In these catastrophic changes, which are occurring in so many families, many people become innocent victims of the decisions of others. Children cannot prevent the divorce of a parent. A spouse cannot always prevent the infidelity of his or her marriage partner. Judges often make the decisions regarding child custody. Death, financial disaster, and severe illness are also unavoidable factors which may disrupt or destroy a family. And while we do have a certain degree of choice, we cannot completely eradicate the influences of a society which seems to place less value on the permanency of marriage and the family than it did a few years back.

Not long ago in my counseling office, a twelve-year-old girl announced with caution, "When I marry I'm going to get a legal paper saying that anything which is mine will never be legally shared with my husband—just in case we get a divorce!" Sandy had just seen her parents go through a rough, unfair divorce proceeding, and so I understood.

Another child of about the same age recently told me that there was no way she would ever get married, and certainly she would not have children. She ended with, "I would never want to put my children through what my parents have done to me and my sister." How sad to be so young and to trust so little in a world which has so far offered them so little choice and so much insecurity and change!

Why all this destructive change in the family? Theologians might call it sin; sociologists might tag it as the demise of an outdated institution; psychologists could label it pathology. But from where I see it, a great fundamental cause of the tearing apart of the family structure is the impact of other massive changes in our society.

For change, whether good or bad, always causes unrest. It is scary to watch one's life change, even from one's own choice. And when those changes come unbidden from a world in turmoil around us, the emotional impact can be terrifying. One result is stress, which is usually directed first and foremost toward those we love, our family. Home is where we feel most uninhibited, and that is where we too often vent our frustration. In this way the family, which has the potential of becoming one of our greatest safety zones, often becomes the casualty of change instead.

One of the greatest changes which has occurred in our world viewpoint is a helpless attitude toward guarantees of our existence—not only for ourselves but for our children and the whole human race. The potential for cosmic annihilation has never been greater. When commercials come on the TV screen advertising plans of escape in case of nuclear attack, most of us feel a sense of futility. Sure, we want a way of escape. But what if we don't survive long enough to even use the plan? Or worse, what if we survive only to die a slow death from nuclear fallout?

War used to be confined to a small part of the world—we hoped not our part. But World War II ended that when the atomic bomb was developed and dropped over Japan. Now we just pray that the whole world isn't burned up.

It is easy to slip from such fears to an almost fatalistic attitude toward family, commitment, and indeed the permanence of anything. When I worked with drug addicts during the time of the Vietnam War, I was frequently told, "I don't care if I destroy my body with drugs; I'll just die in Vietnam anyway." A late twentieth-century counterpart of that viewpoint might well be, "Why commit oneself to anyone when we're all going to burn up in a nuclear holocaust anyway?"

What is important to realize is that more than ever, during threatened annihilation, we need closeness and permanency in human relationships. We need family and friends as a safety zone.

For even though the family in general may be a major casualty of the changes around us, that battered institution can also become one of the main sources of our recovery. It can become a major safety zone.

We may never have all the answers to the issues which technology and social change have brought. We may never eradicate the possibility of a nuclear war. We may not be able to restore the family to its old place of stability in our society. But we can learn to cope with the fast-moving world in which we live through the use of our own family structure, as well as through long-term relationships with friends who support us.

In these matters we do have an element of choice. For while we may not have chosen many of the changes which have occurred around us, we can still choose our attitude toward them. The safety zone of family and even friends will not provide the whole answer to our problems with change, nor will they provide the only way to cope. But for a large number of people, a renewal of family life which is satisfying and sound could become a firm anchor in the turbulence in which we live.

Swiss psychiatrist Paul Tournier underlines this point as he tells of a young student who consulted him. After being raised in something less than an ideal home, the young man said to Dr. Tournier, "Basically I'm always looking for a place—for somewhere to be." Explains Dr. Tournier:

> The ideal place for the child is the family. When I questioned him on the subject, my student friend told me that he had happy memories of his childhood and youth. But upon analysis all his happy memories proved to be situated outside his home. When the family is such that the child cannot fit himself into it properly, he looks everywhere for some other place, leading to a wandering existence, incapable of settling down anywhere. His tragedy is that he carries about within himself this fundamental incapacity for any real attachment. He bears with him his constant, increasing, and unsatisfied nostalgia. He feels he is repulsed, excluded, or ignored. His personal contacts with others are merely conventional and impersonal . . . .
>
> The child who has been able to grow up harmoniously in a healthy home finds a welcome everywhere. In infancy all he needs is a stick placed between two chairs to make himself a house, in which he feels quite at home. Later on, wherever he goes, he will be able to make any place his own, without any effort on his part. For him it will not be a matter of seeking, but of choosing.[1]

In my opinion, this ability to find a home, a place of comfort and safety, is ideally developed in childhood, but it can also to some degree be developed in adulthood. For any adult can work at building his own family, or even a support system of friends, and thereby find a place, a safety zone in the middle of a changing world.

Another area of change which is fundamentally affecting our lives is our long-time friend, medicine, which used to be a sort of sacred cow. On one hand, doctors and hospitals and researchers are doing an even more effective job of saving lives. But modern medicine also poses its threats to our sense of ethics, if not our very existence.

For example, it used to be legitimate to use every available means to save a loved one's life. The boundaries were clear. Now physicians and laymen alike are frightened by the potential to maintain life. We have to pull tubes in order for people to die who would have died long ago without life-sustaining machines. Who makes the decisions? Upon what basis do they make them? What is death? And, for that matter, what is life?

Death thus becomes a source of greater than usual conflict. While death has always involved some guilt for the living, the guilt factor increases when you have to debate over when someone is dead, whether you should cut off a life-sustaining machine or even start the use of one, and if you should force feed or not. And all along, feeding the tension even more, may be the nagging fear that this person who is supposed to be a "vegetable" by now may just be enduring some form of torture, longing to be released. You can't win. It is possible to have little idea of when you're prolonging a life in a torturous existence or when you're actually committing murder.

In recent days I have noticed that when certain professionals talk about an issue like euthanasia, they do not refer to it as "killing." Even the use of the old term, *mercy killing*, seems out of vogue, and they would violently recoil from the word *murder*. Rather, euthanasia is referred to as "the final step in the treatment of the terminally ill."

In my opinion, it is dangerous to tone down the language of an act like euthanasia. It makes it too easy to then accept it as something less than killing a person. It makes it too easy to then perform the act, first on those who choose it and eventually on all those whom society at that time would prefer to be rid of. At that point, one would have to ask oneself, "What is the difference between euthanasia and the gas ovens of Auschwitz or Dachau?"

I understand very deeply the feelings of those who want euthanasia accepted as a viable choice for the terminally ill. But as well as believing that such a choice is opposed to Scriptural teaching, I also feel that to start accepting euthanasia as valid at any level would be to accept a precedent which could have frightening ramifications. It is always dangerous to set a precedent for issues which can then become dangerous tools in the hands of those who have no ethics.

Thus death, an already tense and sometimes destructive time for a family, now presents the added pressure of a mandatory choice which may cause deep avenues of disagreement between family members at a time when that family may already be overburdened with the sense of loss which accompanies the death or potential death of a loved one. For even though euthanasia is not at this time a legal option, families and individuals are still confronted with choices relating to the extent to which a person is to be treated. How much more terrible to have to say, "I just had the tubes pulled on Uncle Ned" than to say, "Uncle Ned passed away in his sleep."

We now have choices in these matters, but fundamentally the whole issue of more precisely defining death and its ethics has been forced upon us by medical technology. The situation is paradoxical. We have no choice about making choices! For even no choice becomes a choice by default!

When my Aunt Lydia died a short while ago, I was confronted with this issue in a way I had never experienced before. The battle I fought within myself in that coffee shop was one of the hardest struggles I have ever undergone. The question which had been posed to me was: "Should we do heroics if she stops breathing; should we use machines and heart massage to bring her back?"

My immediate reaction to that question was Yes. My next reaction was to make no decision at all; after all, what did I know about all this? But then I realized that I had no choice about making a decision. For in this case, to make no decision would automatically be a choice in itself to do the heroics.

Before I went off by myself to think and pray, people said things to me like: "She's eighty-nine, let her go." "What would she want? Go by that." "You don't want her to suffer, do you?" What scared me so much in what was said were the implications that when we reach old age our lives cease to have value, or that avoidance of suffering is a valid criterion for deciding how far to go in trying to save a life, or that we have a right to die when we want to. It was with these kinds of troubled thoughts that I went off to be by myself.

As I sat in that coffee shop, I realized more fully than ever that there were no easy answers and that all of this medical technology which we have at our fingertips, so to speak, has not yet been thought through sufficiently from an ethical-spiritual point of view. And I don't remember a single incident in my life when I have felt such relief and rest in knowing that God does guide in these matters and that He would not fail me now. The will of God became my safety zone in this crucible of choice.

As I thought, I remembered something I had first heard when I was in my teens from a Bible teacher who used to come from England every few years. His name was Alfred J. Crick, and for me he was a dear friend and the source of some very basic biblical teaching. He was fond of repeating, "The Bible is a book of principles." He said it over and over again. Now, in that coffee shop, those words made sense to me in a new way. There was no chapter and verse in the Bible which told a person what to do in my situation. But there were biblical principles upon which I could base my decision. These biblical principles became my safety zone.

As I thought further, I realized that for me the only real matter at stake was God's will. What did He want regarding my aunt's life? Apart from that will of God, neither

Aunt Lydia nor I had a choice we would care to exercise. I knew she would agree with me on this, and that knowledge became another important safety zone.

It then occurred to me that in the area of medical ethics there are at least three fundamental issues at stake. The first issue is euthanasia or mercy killing. As we have just noted, this is not yet a full-blown issue in this country because of our laws against it, nor did it really relate to my aunt's case. However, the popularity of a book like Betty Rollins's *Last Wish,* in which a daughter describes how she helped her dying mother commit suicide, makes it clear, to me at least, that euthanasia could become an issue we might have to deal with in the near future. Already in Holland, for example, the legalization of euthanasia is a major issue.

The next question which came to my mind concerned the morality of refusing treatment. At first I thought that this was what I would be doing by refusing medical heroics. This area seems to me to be a sticky, middle-of-the-road kind of issue. The perimeters seem fairly clear. To refuse a life-saving injection of penicillin because one wishes to die could be considered tantamount to suicide. On the other hand, to continue painful treatments when a patient is not responding and is going to die anyway could be to deny that person the dignity of death and any usable time he or she might have leading up to that death. In between these two extremes, the lines are less distinct to me. But before one makes a decision to refuse treatment it would seem vital to consider the will of God above one's own feelings and desires. In a society which places such a great emphasis on doing what makes one feel good and accommodating one's concept of God to the notion that God Himself exists solely for our convenience and pleasure, it is of particular importance to put a priority on doing the will of God.

It is vital at this point to realize that it is consistent with scriptural truth to say that all of life has meaning—even, and maybe especially, during the difficult times. After speaking of the more obvious forms of meaning in life, Dr. Viktor Frankl says,

For life proves to be basically meaningful even when it is neither fruitful in creation nor rich in experience. . . . [This] group of values lies precisely in a man's attitude toward the limiting factors upon his life. His very response to the restraints upon his potentialities provides him with a new realm of values which surely belong among the highest values. Thus an apparently impoverished existence—one which is poor in creative and experiential values—still offers a last, and in fact the greatest, opportunity for the realization of values. These values we will call attitudinal values. What is significant is the person's attitude toward an unalterable fate. The opportunity to realize such attitudinal values is therefore always present whenever a person finds himself confronted by a destiny toward which he can act only by acceptance. The way in which he accepts, the way in which he bears his cross, what courage he manifests in suffering, what dignity he displays in doom and disaster, is the measure of his human fulfillment. . . . A man's life retains its meaning up to the last—until he draws his last breath- -as long as he has consciousness, he has responsibleness.[2]

Later Dr. Frankl concludes,

Must we not ask ourselves now whether we are ever entitled to deprive an incurably ill patient of the chance to "die his death," the chance to fill his existence with meaning down to its last moment, even though the only realm of action open to him is the realizing of attitudinal values— the only variable the question of what attitude the patient, the "sufferer," takes toward his suffering when it reaches its climax and conclusion? The way he dies, insofar as it is really HIS death, is an integral part of his life; it rounds that life out to a meaningful totality.[3]

What was liberating to me, however, was to finally realize in this process of thinking that the decision I had to make regarding my aunt involved a third issue: whether or not to pull her back *from* death. If she stopped breathing, should the doctors bring her back?

A sudden sense of peace swept over me as I realized that, given her crumbling bones, which were practically paper-thin from osteoporosis, and the general deterioration which was visibly occurring in her body, if God took her it would be immoral to try to bring her back. That would amount to bringing her back *from* death, not preventing her death, and there is a vast difference between the two. For the concept that God is ultimately in charge of the span of our lives is a basic principle which can be seen through the whole Bible.

That principle became a major safety zone for me that evening. I went back to the hospital and requested that a "no code" (no heroics) be put on her chart. A short time later the Lord took her—*in His time.*

As I stood in Aunt Lydia's room moments after her death and looked at the precious remains of one who had deeply loved and served the Lord, I had a deepening sense that she was present with the Lord. She had gone to be with Him in His timing, and for that in particular I rejoiced. For her, the process of dying had been neither prolonged nor speeded up. As a statement of the great struggle to ensure that timing, the inscription on the tablet on her grave reads simply, but with a depth that the average bystander will not fully understand: "The Lord gave, and the Lord hath taken away; blessed be the name of the Lord" (Job 1:21). In His time!

At the other end of the spectrum, we have as much difficulty with life and its beginnings as we do with its ending. We read literature on the impressions a fetus receives from the music which the mother listens to, and then we hear it said that human life doesn't really begin until birth. If that contradiction sounds confusing to us adults, just imagine the impact it must have on an unmarried, pregnant, teenage girl. I have heard stories of babies aborted, lying on the table, kicking, alive. These are babies which if they had been prematurely delivered would have been saved by all the heroics of the medical profession. Yet they are allowed to die because they are considered to be just aborted fetuses.

In recent years, Congress has considered declaring that life legally starts at conception—this after one million abortions performed between 1973, when a Supreme Court decision legalized abortion, and 1983. If and when the 1973 decision is reversed (and perhaps reversed back again) what about these million mothers and their families? Are they to feel that they have killed a viable human being? Are families once again to be torn apart by guilt and confusion?

According to the director of one feminist health center, "The anti-abortion pressure affecting women is greater now than it was ten years ago. It is making women more fearful beforehand and more worried afterwards." The confusion is illustrated by a woman having her seventh abortion at the clinic since the Supreme Court legalized abortion ten years before.

"The seventh," she said, "would not be as easy as the first." She said she still believes that what she is doing is right. But she admitted that the issue is no longer "black and white" for her.

"I cannot help but feel somewhat torn apart," she added. "The moral issue is a bit shaky. Whether it's murder or not. Yet, it's got to be done."

While the procedure was taking place, she said, she would whisper the same silent apology she has offered before, particularly the last few times.

"I don't ask God to forgive me. But I always do say to that small scrap of potential human being that I am sorry and hope that it will come back at a time when it is more appropriate."[4]

Such issues tear a family apart. What once seemed like a sophisticated choice now seems to have gone all wrong, at least in the eyes of many. And we all know by now how quickly that viewpoint can change again. Yet while it changes, girls do get pregnant, babies are aborted, and families reap the effect of the confusion.

A seventeen-year-old girl I know prided herself on being mature enough to be on the pill at an early age, since she knew she was going to be sexually active. While her parents wished she had waited for sex until she was married, they respected her for not taking chances with becoming pregnant. Now that pride is gone and her mother for the first time openly calls her daughter a "slut." The mother had an abortion years ago in what she thought was a wise decision. Now she views her own action with shame. Neither mother nor daughter has yet seen that their feelings of guilt and confusion relate to the changing values which have been occurring around them. They just feel disillusioned in themselves and each other, and the chasm between them widens.

In areas such as sexual morality, there is little stability of thought if we depend upon the changing mores of the society in which we live. It is here, however, that the Christian has an unchanging safety zone. For our God is the One who never changes, and He has given us biblical principles upon which to base our lives.

In the area of abortion, the deciding issue seems to lie in a determination of when life begins. I know Christians as well as non-Christians who believe that life starts when a baby takes his first breath, or when the baby is fully formed in the womb. To me, however, the Scriptures are more clear than that. In the Psalms we read,

You made all the delicate, inner parts of my body, and knit them together in my mother's womb. Thank you for making me so wonderfully complex! It is amazing to think about. Your workmanship is marvelous—and how well I know it. You were there while I was being formed in seclusion! You saw me before I was born and scheduled each day of my life before I began to breathe. Every day was recorded in your Book (Ps. 139:13–16 LB).

For the Christian there is a psychological soundness in a basic code of ethics which remains. In a time of such great unavoidable change it becomes a very important safety zone.

Closely related to the changes in sexual morality are the changes in male and female roles. Feminist Betty Friedan has stated the situation very well in an interview with *Vogue:*

> Twenty years ago, in my generation, women turned their backs on their potential for careers and chose to get complete fulfillment through marriage and children. Now, unless we get on with the second stage, there are going to be a lot of lonely women who seek their whole fulfillment in careers, short-changing or denying their own needs for love and nurturing.

As a general solution to the problem, Ms. Friedan continues:

> I think women can have it all. I think they can have children, they can have love, and they can have their professions, IF they work out trade-offs over time in their own lives and get some simple new arrangements at home and at work. But there has to be flexibility. You can have it all, if you don't try to be Superwoman at the office and Supermom at home.[5]

However, with the increase in divorce and single parenting, it's not all that easy. If women who want it all find it hard to combine so many roles, you can imagine how difficult it is for women who do not want it all but suddenly find themselves working full time and raising children alone, whether they like it or not! Increasingly, too, men fight for child custody—and I am a firm believer in male custody if the father happens to be a more fit parent than the mother. However, not having been raised with child-rearing as a major expectation, some men find themselves temporarily overwhelmed by the task once they have it. Job success, which for men has always been a traditional safety zone and therefore a basic ingredient ir their self-esteem, may deteriorate as their focus shifts from job to home.

Women, on the other hand, felt inadequate a few years ago if they weren't actively pursuing a career. Now first pregnancies are "in" for women in their late thirties and early forties to compensate for what many of these career women realize they still want.

Ms. Friedan says that it is a cruel decision if one has to choose between family and career. To me, that sounds as though she has found out that a career isn't everything, and she can't handle the thought that women might have to make a choice to give up a family if they choose a career. I agree that it is a cruel choice, a choice which for economic and social reasons most women before us have not had to make. But in spite of the pain involved, I'm beginning to believe that such a choice must often be made if one is to avoid the even greater pain of trying to be all things to all people—and then ending up in failure because it can't be done. I believe it is possible to have a career and be a good mother at the same time—possible, but not easy. And ultimately some of the little extras of child-rearing or the push for job promotion will suffer.

Changes in what is expected of us as women or men are disorienting, however. When I was in college, marriage and the family were probably the primary emphasis for a woman, although higher education and career were acceptable. Then, once I was firmly established in a career, a career became the "in" thing and babies were "out," so to speak. Now, both are in, with career coming first and then babies. The pattern will undoubtedly change again soon.

Those of us who have kept our sanity throughout these changes have in general gone on with priorities in the areas of our greatest interests. For many of us, that has included the safety zone of finding out and fulfilling the will of God for our lives. It is not that we have not wanted to do everything, but we have felt the need to make choices.

Not long ago I watched a television interview with a retiring Catholic Archbishop. He was asked about those things, such as family, which he had given up for his life in the church. His answer was positive: he did not regret his choices, and he considered his life work to have been a gift from God.

So might we all consider the place of God's appointment to be a gift, rather than feeling that we have somehow given up too much or been deprived. For in a time of constant changes in male-female roles and in a day when there are endless choices instead of one stereotyped role, we all have to give up some things which we may want to do. All of which brings us back once again to the safety zone of the will of God.

It has been said that F. B. Meyer, the remarkable preacher of a few decades back, was once crossing over in a boat from England to the rugged coast of Ireland during the black of night. He was startled to note that even in the dark the captain was able to know exactly where to turn the ship in toward land. When the captain was questioned about this, he pointed out that there were three lights on the shore, and that when those three lights were in a line he knew that he was going straight into the harbor.

F. B. Meyer saw a great symbolism here regarding the will of God for the believer. The first light represents the biblical principle that God will never reveal to an individual personally that which will conflict with what He has already revealed in His Word. The second light stands for the principle that we must accept up front whatever God reveals to us in His will, before that will is even shown. This means having a permanent mindset for the will of God. The third light involves letting God govern the circumstance rather than what we feel or want or what we feel is fair. When these three lights are together we have the safety zone of the perfect will of God.

Long before the crashing changes of the late twentieth century, but recently enough to see some of them coming, columnist Walter Lippman said, "No mariner ever enters upon a more uncharted sea than does the average human being born in the twentieth century."[6] The sea may indeed be more uncharted than ever, but above all of the chaos of unavoidable change stands our unchangeable God. And in contrast to the vast, uncharted sea is the safety zone of His perfect, dependable will.

Chapter
Four

'Til Death
Do Us Part

It was a hot Sunday afternoon in August as I was going through my mother's things following her death, I came across a box of old letters. My first impulse was to pack them away with other papers I was saving to read someday when I had less to do. Then I noticed that most of the letters had been written from my father to my mother from Seattle during the time span of October 1941 to January 1942.

While he had been originally hired to work in California, for those three months my father had been located in Seattle as an engineer, designing airplanes for Lockheed. His job had been the reason for our recent move from Chicago to California, and while he was in Seattle my mother, my sister, and I had lived in Eagle Rock, California. During that time he had written to my mother almost every day, always including a personal note to my sister and me.

On the August afternoon when I found those letters, a few lines caught my attention. Then the rest of the day slipped by as I was pulled back in time to a marriage based on a commitment which made it a safety zone for my parents as well as for us children.

At the time the letters were written, I had been three and my sister ten. Yet as I read those letters some forty years later, I was the same age as their author had been. Through them, I came to know my parents in a new way, not so much as my parents but just as people.

Times in the 1940s were not easy. All of Europe was

caught up in war, and our country was just emerging from the Great Depression. Then in December 1941 came the bombing of Pearl Harbor, and the United States became directly involved in World War II. The changes were catastrophic and the implications for all of us were intensely personal.

This came through clearly in my father's letters. Although previously he had written about extra money he was putting away to buy a house, in his letter dated 7 December 1941 my father shifted his emphasis to one of personal sacrifice: "I suppose you have heard that Japan has declared war on us. This means we must all do our bit to defend our country. We must sacrifice any selfish motives for our beloved United States." Then, four days later: "Everything up here is on a war basis. I received orders today stating that we are not to leave until our work is done, which will take about two more months. This is bad news, I know, but for the defense of our country it is very necessary. We must win this war, and to do it we must sacrifice."

The war affected us in the many small, practical ways that a child in particular remembers. I vividly remember running with my sister and mother to a place of shelter before all the lights would go out. I remember with awe the Japanese internment camps, with the barbed wire and the guards, for some of our friends were in those camps. I remember debates over how best to use our limited amounts of sugar; and later, after my father had come back to California, I remember the afternoon when he went to every candy store in town trying without success to find some bubble gum for a special treat. In our own family, added to the external changes were all the problems arising from our recent relocation from Chicago. Money was scarce, and our family and friends were two thousand miles away.

Yet in spite of the problems of those early days, as I read my father's letters on that Sunday afternoon I was reminded anew of the sense of commitment both he and my mother had always shown to both their marriage and their family. In the middle of stormy changes both in their personal lives and in the world around them, they *chose* a commitment to each other which became a safety zone in the middle of change. They could not alter the state of the world; they could not quickly improve their own circumstances; but they could and did choose their attitude toward these unalterable circumstances.

Looking back over those years when I was growing up, I never remember my mother's complaining about my father's long work hours, and I never remember even once doubting the permanence of their marriage. They worked around each other's needs and tried to make life easier for each other. They argued, and as I grew up I certainly had my disagreements with them. But never once did I doubt their love for me or for each other. They were there, seemingly forever.

In spite of the changes created by the war, my parents chose to protect us children from as much of the uncertainty as they could. That attitude, too, became a safety zone. They couldn't stop the war for us, but they did make it less scary. They generally chose small ways to buffer the change. My mother often read to me for hours—stories that had an influence on my entire life. She also had a way of making a bad day at least tolerable by the addition of something special. Rainy days became days for favorite foods, and a trip to the dentist might be followed by the purchase of some small toy or book.

In his own way, my father's actions were consistent with those of my mother. The day after Pearl Harbor was attacked, my father wrote to my sister asking her how school was going and if she had been to see Santa Claus yet. In the same letter, he asked me if I was enjoying a toy dog which he had sent me, and he promised to get me a real one some day. (He did!) To even care about such trivia in the middle of the changes which were occurring in his life at this time required choosing the attitude that life would go on normally whenever that was possible.

One of my fondest childhood memories goes back to a time shortly after the outbreak of World War II when my father was back in California but often had to be away for long hours at a time with his work at Lockheed. On some nights when he came home after working late at night he would check my sister's and my room to see if we were still awake. If we were—and I for one made a major effort to stay awake—he would take my mother and us to Bob's Big Boy drive-in restaurant, where we would order milkshakes and hamburgers in the middle of the night.

Perhaps because such a midnight rendezvous would have been normally forbidden, it was such good fun. And in the middle of all of the terrible things which we were hearing about military invasions and Nazi concentration camps, it gave us children, and perhaps all of us, a feeling of hope that someday again life would be normal. Most of life in the early forties was deadly serious. But during these brief interludes we did not worry about what was happening in the world around us, for we had a safety zone in our family which made us feel protected from our changing world.

Upon this background of memory, forty years later I could read my father's letters and understand something of the fabric of a family which had endured, regardless of how many outside pressures converged upon it. As I read, I was reminded of the wedding ceremony which had started all of this and epitomized its basis.

It was a fall day in Chicago at the small Mission Covenant Church. There was only my Aunt Esther; my uncle-to-be, Blanton Jones; the minister; and my mother and father. My mother was dressed in a simple white dress and wore a lovely veil with pearl beading. Another aunt was in China. My maternal grandmother was very ill, and for one good reason or another no one else from the family was able to attend.

As Harry Lindbloom, the elderly Swedish pastor, looked at my mother, he commented, "You look so lovely, it's a shame we don't have more people . . . " Then softly, as though half speaking to himself, he concluded, "But never mind, we have the angels as our witnesses."

And so the marriage began. If it is true that some marriages are made in heaven, then this one certainly was. And it was made to last, for better or for worse, " 'til death do us part," because that is what they both chose.

In a way that is vital to any discussion of safety zones, choice can be used to limit the forces of outside change. As it relates to my family during World War II, for example, the power of choice was the one factor which enabled our family to survive the enormous changes which were affecting us but were beyond our power to eradicate. The ability to choose one's attitude in the middle of unchanging circumstances is to have the potential to develop safety zones.

My parents could not change the external circumstances under which they were forced to start a marriage and a family. But they could choose the kind of commitment to each other which made it possible for that marriage to become a safety zone in the middle of change rather than a casualty of that change. In the same way today, in the middle of a total upheaval in the family structure in general, in any single marriage the same potential for choice remains.

In her book, *The Irrational Season,* Madeleine L'Engle defines the basis of her marriage and her family:

Thirty years ago on a cold morning in January—very cold, it was 18 degrees below zero—when Hugh and I made those vows we were deliberately, if not consciously, leaving youth and taking the risk of adulthood and a permanent partnership. I knew there would be more than glorious nights, longed-for babies, someone to come home to. I knew that an actor and a writer are a poor risk. But we had committed ourselves, before a God neither of us was at all sure about, that we wouldn't quit when the going got rough. If I was not fulfilled by my relationship with this particular man, I wouldn't look around for another. And

71

vice versa. No matter how rough the going got, neither of us was going to opt out.

And later she adds,

If we commit ourselves to one person for life this is not, as many people think, a rejection of freedom; rather, it demands the courage to move into all the risks of freedom, and the risk of love which is permanent; into the love which is not possession but participation.[1]

It is this choice of commitment in a marriage which provides the basis for a strong safety zone in a marriage— a safety zone which not only involves the couple, but which will extend to the children and, indeed, many who become involved with such a family.

When the family unit is truly functioning as a safety zone, it becomes a place of refuge and comfort. It does not become a cave in which to permanently hide from the world. But it does provide temporary safety and thereby a place to gather up one's resources to once again face the challenges of life.

Sometimes in order for something to be successful as a safety zone, there must be a certain amount of structure involved. It doesn't just happen, even with commitment as a basis. One man I know who travels constantly because of his job regularly takes an hour a week to be alone with *each* of his four children. This is a time when he and the child can talk; bat a ball around; go out for a coke; or, if he is out of town, chat on the phone.

To these children, their father provides more of a safety zone than many fathers who come home every night at six and bury themselves in the newspaper. This same man also sets aside a specific time each week for his elderly mother who lives with them. And when he is not out of town, the time after dinner is automatically spent with his wife. That is their own unique safety zone.

There are times, of course, when this routine is broken, for otherwise its rigidity would just contribute more stress to an already busy life. But it is amazing to me how often this man does keep to the routine he has established, for it provides a sense of security for him also in the middle of a lifestyle which is otherwise highly unpredictable.

Providing safety zones in the middle of unalterable change demands choice. It does not just happen; nor is it, of course, limited in scope to the family. There are many other possibilities for the development of safety zones.

One area of potential is that of tradition. We think automatically of the father in *Fiddler on the Roof*, shouting "Tradition!" as his world crumbles around him. We, too, might well shout, "Tradition!" as we see our values challenged and feel the impact of the constant mobility of those whom we thought would always be physically at our sides.

That first Christmas after our family moved to California was a bleak one materially. My father's work with Lockheed had just started, so money was scarce. My father was away a good deal of the time, and my mother missed her family in Chicago. Shortly before Christmas, my parents and we children went Christmas shopping—really more window shopping. It was exciting. Christmas music was playing, and merchants were displaying their wares in as attractive a way as possible.

As we were walking through a large department store, I saw the most beautiful little Christmas tree I had ever laid my eyes on. It was about a foot tall, made of green fuzzy paper interspersed with tiny colored lights. Actually, the "lights" were just little pieces of glass which lit up from the reflected light of a regular light bulb inside the tree. But to me at the age of four, in an era when technology was not as advanced as it is today, this lighted Christmas tree was almost magic and embodied all of the beauty of the Christmas season. I wanted it desperately!

At first my father thought an expenditure of this type was about the last thing we needed that Christmas. Then, a little reluctantly and with some persuasion from my mother, he bought me the tree. For the rest of my childhood and well into my adulthood that tree became a tradition. Every Christmas it sat in the corner of the dining room in a little alcove. Then one year it developed an electrical short and was relegated to a stack in the garage of those things which were bad enough to get rid of but dear enough not to throw away.

Years later, after my mother's death, it was once again a short time before Christmas, and I was going through the things in that same garage. It was a sad task that made the forthcoming Christmas seem increasingly painful in view of the losses which had been sustained that year.

Then, in the corner of the garage, sitting with some old papers and boxes set aside as trash, I spotted it: my little green tree, still intact, if not serviceable. A flood of memories came back of the department store resplendent in all of its Christmas decorations right before the bombing of Pearl Harbor. But most of all came memories of a childhood which was secure in an insecure world.

In the year that my mother died, I had the tree rewired and its stand repainted—red, because red is a happy holiday color! Every Christmas since that time, the little green tree has stood in my dining room at Christmas once again and given cheer to new generations of children who visit. For me it is a safety zone at Christmas. It is the catalyst for a whole group of wonderful memories of the past, set in with newer things which speak of the present. It is a tradition.

There are countless traditions in this world, and each of us has his own set of important ones. They are important to us, for they become safety zones. For me, with my Swedish background, celebrating Christmas on Christmas Eve, eating *lujtfisk* (dried cod soaked in lye!), even though I've never liked it, and making *pepparkokar* Christmas cookies because I *do* like them are all traditions. For most of us, things like birthday candles and waffles on Sunday morning are small bits of trivia with which we have become familiar, and so they have become traditions in our lives. They have become old and reliable ways of living.

It is perhaps in the blending of the old with the new that traditions offer the greatest safety zone. Then, as we receive comfort and reassurance from the past, we can best bear to face the unknown of the future with all of its unavoidable change.

We human beings are such extremists at times. We either preserve the old until it crumbles into dust in our very fingers or we tend to act as though the past has no value to us. We often see the extremes brought out in people at a time of death—in other words, at times of great change. One of my patients who had lost several relatives in a short span of time was understandably weary by the time she had finished going through her mother's things. In her discouragement, she gave away or even threw away all but a few items which the family kept. "I'm glad to get rid of it all and forget" was her comment. Then, a few months later, when her body had somewhat healed from its fatigue, she lamented, "If only I had kept some of those small things that now would remind me of my mother, for I miss her so." She had thrown away a safety zone, and so she had to choose others.

In contrast, after the death of my father, my mother knew that she was in no condition to make balanced decisions. Then, months later, when she could bear to relinquish a bit of the past, she decided what she would do. She would keep the house that she and my father had lived in for over thirty years and the furniture they had brought with them from Chicago. But to make her feel as though she was not just living in the past, she painted the house and reupholstered the furniture.

After my mother's death I remembered her example, and I, too, reupholstered the same furniture, even though at that time it didn't really require it. I needed to keep and lovingly use the sofa and chairs that held so many memories for me. But I needed them as new also, so that I, too, felt I was going forward rather than back.

Some places tend to become reservoirs of the past and as

such provide one with an occasional sense of security. I suppose that is one reason why some people find a great sense of relaxation in museums and art galleries. I myself find this feeling in libraries, for although I don't want to sound maudlin, to me books are friends and as such become great sources of inspiration and comfort. You can go anywhere in a book, and at times you can get to know people from the past far better than many of their contemporaries did. Sometimes I just look at the several thousand books in my own home library and enjoy remembering what some of them have said to me before.

Then I get certain moods to reread certain books. Some are somewhat cyclical, like the mood I have every few months or so to read from the poems of Robert Browning. One never totally understands Browning, at least I don't, so I usually get something new from him each time I reread his works. I understand that at one time even Browning himself said that when he wrote a certain piece only he and God had known what he meant. Now, admitted Browning ruefully, only God knew! Thus reassured regarding my partial understanding of the man and yet greatly inspired by his thinking, I have enjoyed a safety zone in reading Browning and, of course, others.

All of us have physical places, also, to which we retreat in times of stress. After repeated use, these places become safety zones for us, for they retain a sense of familiarity from the past while also enabling us to go on in the present.

In the little beach town to which I retreat, there is a stately, old hotel where I am particularly prone to go when life's changes become acute. It is familiar to me and therefore comforting and safe, but it is also just plain old and imbued with that feeling of safe antiquity which some of us glean from the past. Many people have apparently felt the same way, for people tend to return, and on one of the walls off of the lobby there are pictures of famous people from the past who have frequented this beach resort.

The hotel is a perfect blending of the old with the new. There are, indeed, the old pictures, the antique furniture, and the really antiquated but charming elevator with its live operator and its walls lined with framed pictures of the past. Yet the hotel is not the least bit musty. The service is superb, and there are little extras which somehow make one feel refurbished by one's stay: Beds turned down at night with a mint and a poem on the pillow, hot chocolate sipped at bedtime on the veranda overlooking the sea, coffee and fruit served in the morning in the room as one awakens and followed by a quick dip in the warm pool if one so chooses—these all contribute to recovery and going on.

In times of stress, a short stay at this hotel is worth more than a longer stay somewhere else—at least to me! For it is *my* safety zone. It might not work for someone else. For safety zones are unique to each of us, although certain principles remain true for all. That which is pleasant and familiar has the potential to be a safety zone for anyone. One's own definition of *pleasant* will vary. However, very often that which is old blended with that which is new makes a very comforting package.

It is perhaps our uniqueness which makes choice such an important factor in the use of safety zones. For not only is individual taste involved, but there is also the importance of individual circumstance. In no area is this seen more than in the area of the family. In my family, for example, when fifteen of us sat down to family dinners, it was appropriate for me to talk about the family as a safety zone for me—but only for me! Those memories still remain as a safety zone which is of great value to me. But my living family, on this earth, is no longer my safety zone. They are gone, and there are many like me who cannot feel anything but depression when they read in books and hear from the pulpit that the family should be their center of life. Generally that may be true, but not always—and not ever for some!

When I was doing my graduate work many years ago, I

lived for two years at the home office of Bethel Mission of China. Betty Hu, the vice president of that mission, lived there, too, with an occasional Chinese student and one American missionary. Betty was, and still is, one of the wisest people I have ever known. In one of her statements of advice, she said to me, "When you don't have a family, you can do one of two things. You can become part of other people's families or you can develop your own."

Betty knew from hard experience what she was talking about, for she had lost her own family and endured much pain during the Japanese wars in China. Her wisdom did not, however, apply to me at that time. Then when I, too, lost all my family her words came back to me. I decided to "make my own family," as she put it, rather than to wander around like a nomad, fitting into everybody else's life. The rewards have been great, and God has given me some wonderful supports in people who, collectively and individually, have become a safety zone for me.

You don't have to have a family to have close relationships which in times of stress become a refuge. For all of our emphasis on family, it is a little ironic to me that in His deepest agony in Gethsemane Jesus Christ took with Him His three closest disciples, not His natural family. Indeed, the emphasis on His earthly relationships, apart from His devotion to His mother, is on people not related by blood, who definitely provided Him with a safety zone, imperfect as that sometimes became.

It is not my purpose in any way to minimize the value of the family. Certainly my work and own life experience go in the opposite direction. But it is possible to so enshrine the natural family as the only viable safety zone that people who have no family become discouraged and hopeless. In the area of family and friends, as in every other area, we have choices. A family can be a wonderful safety zone, but so can friends. And in this area we have the perfect example in our Lord Himself as He walked on this earth.

Ultimately, regardless of our circumstances, we can choose our safety zones, and indeed we must choose them if we are to survive in this world of change. Especially when our circumstances are beyond our choice, we must choose our attitude toward those circumstances. At the risk of overquoting from Dr. Viktor Frankl, an illustration from his *The Will to Meaning* succinctly and poignantly clarifies this point:

A Carmelite sister was suffering from a depression which proved to be somatogenic. She was admitted to the Department of Neurology at the Poliklinil Hospital. Before a specific drug treatment decreased her depression this depression was increased by a psychic trauma. A Catholic priest told her that if she were a true Carmelite sister she would have overcome the depression long before. Of course this was nonsense and it added a psychogenic depression (or, more specifically, an "ecclesiogenic neurosis," as Schaetzing calls it) to her somatogenic depression. But I was able to free the patient of the effects of the traumatic experience and thus relieve her depression over being depressed. The priest had told her that a Carmelite sister cannot be depressed. I told her that perhaps a Carmelite sister alone can master a depression in such an admirable way as she did. In fact, I shall never forget those lines in her diary in which she described the stand she took toward the depression.

"The depression is my steady companion. It weighs my soul down. Where are my ideals, where is the greatness, beauty, and goodness to which I once committed myself? There is nothing but boredom and I am caught in it. I am living as if I were thrown into a vacuum. For there are times at which even the experience of pain is inaccessible to me. And even God is silent. I then wish to die. As soon as possible. And if I did not possess the belief that I am not the master over my life, I would have taken it. By my belief, however, suffering is turned into a gift. People who think that life must be successful are like a man who in the face of a construction site cannot understand that the workers dig out the ground if they wish to build up a cathedral. God builds up a cathedral in each soul. In my soul he is about to dig out the basis. What I have to do is just keep still whenever I am hit by His shovel."[2]

We, like the Carmelite sister, cannot always choose our circumstances. When we are faced with questions regarding how far to let medical technology treat a loved one or what to do with our own children in a society where family values and moral ethics undergo seemingly constant change, we may indeed feel helpless. Yet like the Carmelite sister we, too, can choose our attitude toward our circumstances. We, too, can limit the power of these circumstances over our lives by choices which in themselves, become safety zones. Above all, like the Carmelite sister, we, too, can make God our refuge.

In *Whispers of His Power,* a recently published devotional book compiled from letters and papers previously unpublished, Amy Carmichael quotes from Jeremiah 3:4 with the words of the Septuagint: "Hast thou not called Me as it were a home?" The words are reminiscent of those of St. Augustine when he said: "Thou madest us for Thyself, and our heart is restless, until it repose in Thee."[3] To choose God is to find a true home in this world of constant change. To me the idea of finding a home, a safety zone, in repose in Jesus Christ are perhaps best summed up once again in that old, favorite hymn of Hudson Taylor's:

> Jesus! I am resting, resting
>   In the joy of what Thou art;
> I am finding out the greatness
>   Of Thy loving heart.
> Thou hast bid me gaze upon Thee,
>   And Thy beauty fills my soul,
> For, by Thy transforming power,
>   Thou hast made me whole.
>
> *Jean Sophia Pigott*

I Have a Foxhole In My Mind

When I was growing up, the mountains above our house were a favorite place for me to ramble with my huge Saint Bernard-and-collie dog, Jack, and whomever else I could persuade to go with me. In those days the mountains were untouched by golf courses and restaurants, and tucked back into a lower part of the mountain was a large cave. It was reached by a relatively short mountain path, and by letting my dog Jack run ahead I was fairly safe from any surprise encounter with a snake.

The cave intrigued me. "Who lived there?" I would question. "A bear," I always decided. There really didn't seem to be any bears living in our area. However, the barking of coyotes every night and the more distant yowling of mountain lions reinforced my belief that something real and ferocious must indeed live in "my cave," as I came to call it. Although I speculated a lot about the cave, I never went into it beyond the entrance. It was just too scary.

But at home where it was safe, my friends next door and I tried to make our own cave, of sorts, first by digging a hole which we hoped would go to China (because we had read about that in some book). When we despaired of ever reaching China, we erected an Indian tent, which more completely gratified our "cave" mentality, and we camped out in it until the darkness and the noises of the night scared us and we crept silently back to our own warmer and seemingly safer beds.

Throughout childhood, I had my own special secret

places to which I often retreated alone: my special tree into which I could climb with a good book and be lost to the world for hours; the hidden spot behind the rose garden where the water faucet dripped just enough to make the dirt into the perfect consistency for mud pies; and the big umbrella tree in the back yard, which wasn't all that secret, but nevertheless provided a shady spot on a hot day where my dolls and dog and I could have a picnic.

Caves and secret places in general are captivating to children and to the child in all of us adults. C. S. Lewis appeals to this quality in the *Chronicles of Narnia,* where the initial entry into another dimension comes by exploring an old wardrobe that is so big that a child can enter into it. It is interesting to me that the children in Lewis's books find the wardrobe during a time of stress, when they are staying in the country home of a professor away from the dangers of London and its air raids. It is as though this enchanting wardrobe, with its cavelike interior filled with long fur coats and the smell of mothballs, provides a diversion and thus a safety zone during a time of great external stress.

Other children in literature seem to enjoy secret, hidden, cavelike places: Tom Sawyer had his actual, physical cave. Books like the Nancy Drew mysteries appeal to a child's world of imaginary intrigue and secrecy, a kind of inner cave. The popular "Little House" books are filled with descriptions of haylofts, abandoned shacks, and mossy banks along secluded creeks where children can retreat and recover from the often frightening demands of life around them.

One of the aspects of my mother's life which I envied as a child was the abundance of secret places which she had when she was growing up near the Dells in Wisconsin. She could retreat to an actual woods or fish in a small lake. Her father had built a barn with a hayloft, which provided a perfect hiding place. And she and her sisters often picnicked on the mossy banks of a nearby creek, using a white tablecloth and china dishes, a scene which in all the photographs appears to have a quaint, faintly romantic touch.

A child's fascination with secret places and caves is related to the impulse to run for cover or to pull the blankets up over one's head when one is afraid. Caves and cavelike places represent being hidden, safe, protected. When we are grown up, we become embarrassed over our vulnerability, but I suspect that most of us still have a secret desire for a cave from time to time.

During the closing months of World War II, after he had been catapulted into the presidency by the death of Franklin D. Roosevelt, Harry Truman was asked how he handled the inordinate stresses which had been thrust upon him. According to an article that appeared years ago in *Reader's Digest,* Truman's answer was, "I have a foxhole in my mind. . . ." He explained that, just as a soldier retreats into his foxhole for protection and respite, he periodically retired into his own "mental foxhole" where he allowed nothing to bother him.

The article continues, "He was, in effect, heeding the wisdom of Marcus Aurelius, who wrote: 'Nowhere, either with more quiet or more freedom from trouble, does a man retire than into his own soul.' And because he believed this ability to retire within himself was essential for peace of mind, Marcus Aurelius advised: 'Constantly then give to thyself this retreat and renew thyself.'" In a similar way Truman, too, had his cave, his secret place, his safety zone within himself into which he could retreat, feel safe, refurbish, and then go on.

Places, people, traditions and a myriad of other things can provide each of us with safety zones. But in the positive mental "tapes" which each of us carries around within us, we each have also a foxhole in our minds, a place within ourselves to which we can escape at any time. The positive memories and dreams which lie buried in each of our minds provide the potential for a built-in cave, a safety zone when there may be no external safety zone to run to.

It is not the physical cave of our childhood pursuits, but it fulfills all those childhood needs for comfort and safety from the outside world.

When I lost my Aunt Lydia, one of my safety zones became my memories, my positive tapes, which are mine forever. Things, people, money, power, position—these all can be lost overnight. But memories remain, and if they are used properly they can become one of our most valuable safety zones. Often the tapes of the past are triggered by something very simple: a line of music reminds us of a romantic experience in the past; a whiff of perfume reminds us of someone we knew and liked; the aroma of cookies baking in the oven may remind us of coming home after school on rainy days when we were kids.

In my counseling office I have a huge dollhouse which contains some rather unique dolls and pieces of dollhouse furniture. This dollhouse in itself becomes a wonderful safety zone for many of my younger patients, a sort of pretend cave into which they retreat mentally. On the doll bed in this house are several blue pillows with small, white daisies on them. My mother made them when I was about seven out of what had been my favorite dress. My Aunt Ruth had made the dress when she had come home on furlough from China, and as I started to outgrow it she had added her own handmade tatting to make it longer. When it was well beyond its usefulness as a dress, my mother, unable to give up such a favorite of mine, used it as part of the furnishings for that year's Christmas gift: a dollhouse.

As I grew up I forgot about these pillows, but somehow they were never thrown away. Later, in the middle of losing my whole family, I found these small pillows, and they became a tiny safety zone, a small foxhole in my mind. For when I look at them I remember my aunt and her intricate needlework, my mother and my Christmas present that year so long ago. Most of all, I have a warm sense of all the love that was there. Materially, only the small pillows remain. But the memories which I have when I look at them are positive mental tapes which can never be taken from me. These have comforted me.

No matter how bad or how good our past has been, we all have some positive memories. A friend of mine had polio, and her childhood memories are blighted by the memory of mean nurses, painful tests, and not walking. But she also has memories of kind nurses and the painful but successful process of learning to walk again, even after all medical opinion had said she couldn't. I suspect that being told that she could never walk again provided her best impetus for eventually learning to walk.

One of my friend's worst memories of her hospital experience was the death of her little friend in the next bed. One morning the two children were chatting as usual, then by afternoon the curtains were drawn between them and my friend knew that something terrible had happened. That is a negative tape, stored permanently in her mind, but one which she wisely tries not to play too often.

At the same time, in the middle of all that horror, she has pleasant memories of the kind which seem to be so important to a child but appear trivial to the adult mind. One of them relates to bubble gum, a harder commodity to come by in those days than it is now. The little girl in the next bed, the same one who later died, had a father who owned a candy store. Every day her father brought her bubble gum, and she shared it with my friend. Bubble gum every day, not just now and then: to these two lonely, little girls that was special. After all, in those days the average kid out there didn't get it that often. And so it became a good tape, a happy memory which to this day gives my friend a feeling of warmth about that otherwise bad period of her life.

Good memories can soften our losses. Yet it is important not to live in past, but rather to go on in the present. For if we so enshrine the past that we ignore the present, we will lose the value of the present and, before we know it, it too will be the past. A couple I know who lost their first baby during its first year of life still mourn the child's death to excess and seem almost unaware of their other two children. They are always talking about the months when Jimmy was alive and about how perfect he was.

Someday when their other children are grown up, these parents may suddenly be aware that because they spent too much time playing and replaying the tapes of that lost first child, they actually buried the other two children with him in their minds. They will have so emphasized the lost beauty of their first child that they will have never seen the truly wonderful qualities in the other two. They will have so enshrined the past that they will have been incapable of appreciating the present; and so, in a sense, they will have lost both.

While good memories can be a mental foxhole into which we retreat in times of stress, it is dangerous to retreat too far or for too long. For, once again, we are not meant to live in our safety zones. Not only can we lose the present if we overemphasize the past, but it is also necessary to be selective about *what* memories we choose to play as well as *when* we allow them to play. For much as we tend to feel that we have little or no control over our emotions and thoughts, I believe that we have a great deal of control, far more than we are led to believe.

As I came home from the hospital on the night of my mother's death, memories flooded my mind. But one in particular came to mind with an agonizing potential, and I immediately cut it off as a tape to be played at a later date. It was a memory of a time when I was quite little. My mother and I had gone to an afternoon children's concert to hear "Peter and the Wolf." Somewhere in the middle of the concert, I started to ask my mother a question. She was listening intently to the music; so as I turned, instead of saying anything, I caught myself looking at her face, observing the soft wisps of light brown hair curling around her temples and noting the clear, pink complexion which was the envy of people all her life.

I realized for the first time that each human being is truly unique and irreplaceable. And in a flash moment of painful awareness I knew that some day my mother would be gone from this earth, that I would lose her. For the first time her mortality struck me. I realized there would never again be on this earth a person identical to her, and I realized more fully how very precious she was to me, how lucky I was to have her. Then I stopped the thought process, for it frightened me.

As I remembered this incident right after my mother's death, I knew it was definitely a memory that I wanted to think about later, but not during the first flush of grief. Later, to remember that first awareness of how special she was could be and was constructive; now it could only be harmful. It would not for this moment be a safety zone.

Yet even a few days later at her funeral, I think that those bittersweet childhood memories gently and unconsciously influenced and comforted me. For after the service, I went over to her grave and prayed, thanking God for ever giving her to me, committing her precious human remains to the earth until that day when He should take them to Himself, and rejoicing in the fact then even now she herself was not in that grave but was in His presence. "Absent from the body, present with the Lord" rang joyously through my mind.

Not since childhood had I been so acutely aware of my mother's uniqueness. But this time I was even more aware of the fact that she had eternal life through the blood of Jesus Christ and that she was even at that moment a part of that cloud of witnesses of Hebrews 12 who now surrounded us. That knowledge became one of my greatest safety zones. It was, for those days, a foxhole in my mind.

Positive tapes of the past can provide great comfort from within, a foxhole in the mind, so to speak, a safety zone, but only if they are used selectively at the right time and for a healthy period of time. Furthermore, it is important to always keep adding to our stock of positive tapes from the present.

A short time ago, in the middle of January, we here in California had a sudden change in weather. For a number of days the temperatures soared and even the plants began to bloom prematurely. Supermarkets began to advertise strawberries which had ripened early because of the warmth, and birds began to sing as though it were spring once again. When the weekend came, some friends and I went to the ocean.

The first night as I lay in bed, I absorbed the sound of the waves pounding on the shore, and I deliberately stored the memory in my mind for days when I would be in the city, far removed from the sounds of the sea. As I walked along the shore the next morning and examined the many tidepools which had been left exposed as the tide had retreated, I again memorized the sight, the tranquil pools of water and the distant, sun-soaked sea. For in times of stress such images will provide me with positive tapes of tranquility. They are a foxhole in my mind, a safety zone into which I retreat.

For some, a storehouse of memories of the sea would not satisfy. A tall pine tree or a desert scene would be the source which would provide for them a foxhole in their mind. From these they would preserve memories which in bleaker days would provide refuge and restoration. For each of us is refreshed by scenes which appeal to our individual tastes.

There are also positive tapes which are not just memories but are dreams of the future. Such dreams have frequently been the impetus for greatness. One of the thrills of my college years was meeting and briefly getting to know Gladys Aylward, the "small woman" of the book by Alan Burgess and the courageous missionary portrayed by Ingrid Bergman in the movie, *The Inn of the Sixth Happiness.* Gladys Aylward was an uneducated, unknown woman in England until she decided, against all odds, to go to

China. She didn't even qualify for any of the established missionary societies of the day. And so she went on her own, on the Trans-Siberian Railway, without money, without a knowledge of the Chinese language, to a remote place in the north of China where the people had never seen a white person before. She did a work for God in an area of the world which had not been touched by conventional missions, a work culminating in her now-famous journey to bring one hundred homeless children to safety during the Japanese invasions of China.

Gladys Aylward had a dream which she put into shoe leather, and in addition to doing a great work for God, she found purpose for her own life through this dream. Her reason to be was a safety zone in the middle of a life which, until she had that dream, had no meaning beyond mere survival.

Dreams do not have to be idle, foolish wishes. They can become concrete motivation to do things for God which are beyond what we deemed possible. They can become positive tapes, foxholes in our minds, safety zones which provide the potential for added meaning and focus in our lives. Especially when we add the dimension of God to our dreams, they often become more than dreams; they become reality. And so what was once a safety zone of hope within our minds can now become a safety zone of reality in our lives.

It was early in the year 1951. A young man in the city of Shanghai, China, was becoming increasingly uneasy about the new government, which had stripped the whole country of its former leaders, forcing untold numbers into exile. This was the place of his birth, his home. While he had broken from tradition and become a Christian, he was still very much Chinese. Generations before him had lived and died here. Yet, for the sake of his wife and little girl, was it safe to remain where uncertainty and doubt grew greater with each passing day? Within himself a dream of moving to the free world began to form.

Then one day supplies were needed from Kowloon, a city bordering Hong Kong in free China. Mr. Chao requested a travel permit from the new government.

"Where is Kowloon?" the official asked him, in a state of obvious confusion over the geography of that great country which his party had so recently seized.

"Near Canton," replied Mr. Chao, hoping against all reason that the officials would not realize that Kowloon, though indeed near Canton, was not in communist China. But his hopes were realized and the permit was granted, a permit which did not specify the number of persons it covered!

After a brief journey to bring back the needed supplies for friends and relatives, Mr. Chao and his small family left for a "vacation" and found refuge in the free world. What began as the comfort of a dream, the hope for freedom, became enabled through faith in God to become the reality of a new start in the free world. The safety zone of hope became the safety zone of fulfillment and success.

For if dreams are a foxhole in the mind which when fulfilled can produce outward success, then the feelings of achievement and fulfillment which come from succeeding also provide an inner safety zone of having done something worthwhile.

On days when my writing seems to drag, for example, the success of what I have written previously which has seemed to help people spurs me on. Focusing on my success helps me ultimately to persevere with what at the moment does not feel successful. Previous achievement becomes a safety zone which provides motivation. In a similar manner, remembering those patients who have solved some of their problems through counseling gives me hope for others who have grown more slowly. The memory of success encourages hope for future success.

A major problem in our society, however, lies in our definition of concepts such as success. To many the meaning of success has deteriorated to power, fame and above all money. If it is true that you can, in part, judge a people by their television commercials, then it would be accurate to assume that our greatest gauge of success at this time is money. If you are rich, you are successful. And, of course, power and fame help in the accumulation of riches. We all get caught up in this attitude, sometimes without even realizing it. We feel that if we are having a hard time financially we aren't "making it," and we have a compulsion not only to keep up with the Joneses but to surpass them.

Last Christmas I was deeply moved by reading Elizabeth Sherrill's article on the composer George Frederick Handel in *Guideposts* magazine. Throughout his life, Handel fought reoccuring indebtedness. At one point, he suffered from a paralyzing stroke which promised, at the age of fifty-two, to end his creative life. His spontaneous recovery from his paralysis has never been understood by doctors. Then, four years after his recovery, he wrote his famous oratorio, *Messiah*, finishing only twenty-three days after he started. As Handel stared at the bulky manuscript, he exclaimed, "I think that God has visited me!"

After its initial success, however, the *Messiah* seemingly lost its popularity. The organized church thought it was sacrilegious to speak of God from a stage rather than from the pulpit, and so the piece was effectively boycotted. Finally, after giving up on paying his debts with the piece, Handel gave it to London's Foundling Hospital, where to this day a handwritten copy of *Messiah* is on display.

Handel then began leading a yearly performance of the *Messiah* in the hospital's chapel. At first, people came to hear this man who was known to be the world's greatest organist. But eventually they came to hear *Messiah*, until the yearly performance became the highlight of the London social season. Handel became blind at the age of sixty-seven, but he continued the performances until his death at seventy-four. In the last years, "as he was led by two children to the organ, the audience would weep with pity. As he began to play, they would weep with joy."[1]

The *Messiah* has never stopped gaining in popularity since that day. Yet Handel never earned one penny from it. His greatest work was one which he gave away to a foundling home, and yet it marks the pinnacle of his success.

An anecdote from the life of Winston Churchill sums up the true meaning of success succinctly:

When Walter Annenberg found himself seated next to Sir Winston Churchill at a stage dinner party given by Bernard Baruch in New York in 1949, he was delighted and somewhat awed. But "about 1 in the morning, after endless wines and beakers of brandy," he plucked up his courage, turned to Churchill and said, "'Sir, I hope you don't think me presumptuous, but I must tell you how saddened I was at the electorate in your country rejecting you as they did after you had saved their empire and their way of life.'" Churchill's reply was: "'Young Annenberg, look not for rewards from others but hope you have done your best.'"[2]

Money, fame, and power can certainly become legitimate ingredients in success. But at its highest level, they are not enough. Hitler had all three at one time—money, fame and power—but he could hardly be said to have experienced true success with its accompanying sense of worth. Many so-called successful people in our present time do not know the safety zone of meaning which arises from knowing, as Churchill put it, that they have done their best. Nor do they experience the safety zone of satisfaction as Gladys Aylward did after she led those hundred children through the mountains of China to a place of safety.

Perhaps, however, the ultimate of success lies not only in actual achievement, even when that achievement is of the noblest quality, but in Churchill's idea of doing your best. The Olympics have honed in to this concept through their emphasis not only on winning, but on trying.

We have seen this same attitude dramatically portrayed in many people's reactions to the tragic end of the *Challenger* space shuttle, when seven promising lives were snuffed out in a matter of seconds.

Was *Challenger* a failure? Certainly it was just that if you gauge success and failure by whether or not the shuttle performed as planned. By that standard it couldn't have failed more effectively. But when you consider the words of the poet James Russell Lowell, "Not failure but low aim is crime," then success and failure take on a whole new perspective. The *Challenger* team gave their absolute, ultimate try, and that, in my definition, is success. Taking the chance to achieve something important was the real success. For as *Challenger's* commander, Francis Scobee, said earlier, the alternative to risk is to go into your bedroom, close the door, and turn off the lights. That is the truest failure.

In his poem, "Rabbi Ben Ezra" Robert Browning says in part:

> All I could never be,
> All, men ignored in me,
> This, I was worth to God, whose wheel the pitcher
>   shaped.[3]

And, consistent with the concept of the safety zone of meaning, Browning adds:

> What I aspired to be,
> And was not, comforts me.[4]

Success is not limited to the fulfillment of dreams. For the dreams themselves, if they are noble, mark us with success. Our very aspiration gives meaning to our lives and can be a safety zone in our mind. The aspiration of the *Challenger* team, rather than the fulfillment of that aspiration, has undoubtedly been a major comfort for their families. Their aspiration is what has been an inspiration to millions of school children. One little girl summed it up when she came home from school and said, "When I grow up, I want to be an astronaut just like them." Their aspiration has now become the dream of a little girl. For her it is a dream of hope. It is her inner cave into which she can retreat when she is discouraged.

Memories of the past, aspirations for the future, the worth of a job well done: all of these can be for each of us a positive tape, a foxhole in our mind, a place where we find hope as well as meaning for our lives. For the Christian, however, the ultimate of inner safety zones is Christ in us. There are countless stories of people imprisoned in totalitarian countries whose storehouse of memorized Scripture became their inner refuge. In less dramatic situations, each of us who knows Christ has experienced the inner power of God to be an anchor in the middle of stress.

Years ago, when I was a young teacher just starting my career in that field, I taught for two years in an excellent private school where discipline was almost never a problem and the students seemed to learn practically on their own. For the first year I was fine. Teaching was new to me, and just knowing that my students were only four years younger than I was ample challenge.

At some point in the second year, however, I became intensely bored. The challenge was gone. I liked teaching, but I wanted the excitement of teenagers who put up some resistance and thereby challenged my skills. As the year went on I began to question my choice of teaching as a career, and I desperately wanted to quit midyear. I hated Mondays and lived for Fridays, and I finally got so desperate that I would have welcomed illness, if it wasn't too severe, over having to go to work.

As I began to reevaluate my life, I realized I didn't doubt the validity of my original decision to go into teaching. But I now knew that I was better suited to the rough-and-tumble existence of a public school. That assessment proved correct, for before I became a family counselor and writer I spent ten happy years teaching at all levels of achievement in a public high school. However, my big problem during that second year of teaching was how to finish the year.

Then one day I was reading an expository book on the Book of Romans, particularly the sixth chapter. Reference was made to the concept of "Christ liveth in me." It was as though the words were illuminated within me. I had seemingly always known them, and yet never known them.

From that day on, until a very successful ending of the school year, Christ in me became my safety zone in a special way. What I couldn't do, He could do. My life became a continuous process of drawing upon His love, His patience, His life. It never became easy until I changed schools. But it became possible. I still didn't like my job that much, but I had an inner peace of knowing the will of God in a way that I had never experienced before. I was in the place of God's appointment, and He was my constant supply. I didn't have to beg Him for what I needed; I simply had to draw from His supply.

"I have a foxhole in my mind." I have an inner cave, like the one I found so many years ago in the mountains above my childhood home. I have a safety zone within. All of these thoughts came to me once again with renewed freshness as I was reading a small, autobiographical book of Hudson Taylor's. In it, Mr. Taylor tells the story of his father who, before Hudson Taylor's birth, began to pray for a son who would go to China. This was in the year 1830, not a time when such a prayer for one's future son could be considered typical! It was a dream, a hope, a safety zone bathed in prayer and in the will of God. When Hudson Taylor was born and grew up with health problems, the dream seemed unrealistic. But, as Hudson Taylor put it, "When the time came . . . God gave increased health, and my life has been spared, and strength has been given for not a little toilsome service both in the mission field and at home, while many stronger men and women have succumbed."[5]

It is a great commentary on the wisdom of Hudson Taylor's parents that their actual dream for his life was not revealed to him until after he had already been in China for seven years.

There was a father's dream, which seemingly would end with aspiration only, not fulfillment. But then there was God. And from that dream was to issue forth not just the hope of a safety zone for one individual, but the founding of one of the greatest missionary endeavors ever to exist.

Chapter
Six

Living Above Our Emotions

When I was in my early teens, a friend of mine lost her father in an airplane crash. Because his work as a pilot kept him away for long periods of time, Lisa had not seen much of her father as she was growing up. Consequently, she had often felt that he didn't love her very much. At the time of the crash, the question of his love burned itself deeply into her consciousness.

Then one day, about a month after his death, Lisa said to me, "You know, if I let my doubts really get to me I'll go crazy. So I'm letting it go."

Letting it go? I thought. *Impossible!* To my way of thinking, one had to find out "the truth," "handle it," and "work it through"—which amounted to a lot of painful, analytical thinking. It would have meant playing old, negative tapes, but I didn't know that then.

Someone once said to me: When the tapes go completely out of control, the person smashes the machine, and that is suicide. For not all tapes are positive. Unfortunately, it seems to be characteristic of human nature not to use the safety zone of good tapes enough. In contrast, we tend to gravitate far too often toward replaying old tapes of unpleasant memories of the past and fearing the "what ifs" of the future.

Negative tapes as well as positive tapes can come in the form of memories. At times, these tapes can start out to be pleasant and, at that point, can be indulged to advantage. The other day, for example, I smelled a delicious coffeecake baking in someone's oven. A flood of memories came back to me once again of Saturday mornings when I was a child and often my first sense of awakening had come through the aroma of my mother's homemade Swedish coffeecake baking. This is a pleasant memory, a good tape. But even good tapes must be guarded. For I could easily let that good memory of childhood drift into a tape on my mother's death. The once-positive tape would now have become a negative one.

Many times, however, the negative aspects of an old tape are more immediately obvious. Going over and over the pain of a divorce, for example, just keeps the experience alive and is tantamount to living through many divorces instead of just one. The same principle is true in handling the memories of a death or rape or the images involved in witnessing a fatal car accident.

It is true that negative experiences need to be reacted to, felt, and talked about. *Feelings* do need to be expressed. But once these feelings have been felt, if they are talked about endlessly, examined, and even feared, at that point they become negative *tapes*. We all know when we are playing negative tapes, even though we may not tag them as such. For old tapes are accompanied by tension, a tightness in one's gut, a sense of agitation or futility.

Nor does an old tape have to be identical to anything we've ever experienced before to qualify as an old, negative tape. I have counseled patients who have a pathological fear of death, for example. When they come in playing a tape regarding whether or not they have AIDS, a disease they never thought about before and have no tangible reason to fear, as a counselor I have to assume that they are playing an old tape—namely, the fear of dying—which has probably been precipitated by something as innocuous as the evening news. Their fear of AIDS is not a new tape; it is just a variation of the old tape concerning death.

When the replaying of negative tapes causes continued tension and anxiety, I have found it best to "cut" the tape and refocus on something positive. For cutting a tape does not work if a new focus is not immediately accomplished. The formula is *cut and refocus.*

It is important, too, for the person to realize that when the tapes are playing hard and the person is at a high peak of anxiety, it may take a while before the negative tape runs down, so to speak. But it *will* run down and stop playing as long as the person maintains the process of cut and refocus. Still, the tape will return from time to time, for no tape is ever truly eradicated. Yet as the process of cut and refocus becomes a part of automatic behavior it will be increasingly possible for the person involved to live beyond the old tapes.

For even psychological counseling can become destructive if it consists of playing old tapes rather than helping the person cut them, in which case the patient may feel consistently worse after a counseling session rather than better. Contrary to popular thought, an endless process of "working through" all the details of a disturbing experience is often more destructive to the individual than it is helpful.

At the extreme, I saw one woman in my counseling office who, following the advice of a professional therapist, had been told to stay home and "work through" her depression. She sat at home trying to feel and understand her depression until it nearly drove her to suicide. My advice to cut the tapes, so to speak, and become active again seemed unsympathetic to her at first. But within two weeks she was back at work feeling incredibly better. Even when her marital problems, which had caused her original depression, eventuated in a divorce, she never again allowed herself to be so completely caged in by her feelings.

In my counseling with molested children I have perhaps seen most dramatically the difference between those who are encouraged to play old tapes and those who are not. Children who are constantly questioned by their parents or a therapist about the experience do not recover as well or as quickly as those who are allowed to go on. And if the therapist repeatedly asks leading questions such as, "Are you sure this only happened once?" or "Your sister said that she was molested; why won't you admit it, too?" the child may actually begin to think that bad things happened in his childhood which never really happened.

I have also seen children who begin to get a "high" from the constant retelling. Being molested has become their claim to fame, the one factor which sets them apart from other kids and makes them feel special. Fostering such an attitude in a child not only damages the child but it sets up an atmosphere in which children can easily begin to think that faking child abuse or child molestation is an easy way to get attention.

In contrast, one ten-year-old child I saw, who had been sexually molested with particular brutality and who was finally happily settled in a foster home where the parents deeply understood her, said to me in her first visit, "I've already talked about what happened to me, and I don't feel like thinking about it any more. I just want to stay where I am, and when I grow up I want to take in children who have been hurt like me." She had learned to cut the tapes of her memories—bad memories whose replaying could only produce the opposite effect from that of a safety zone.

Similar to the tapes which are memories, sometimes a negative tape is just an old way of reacting to a given set of circumstances. The pattern has become routine to us; it has become automatic because of its repeated use. Whether or not the response is a healthy one, it becomes what we always do. It feels like a safety zone, but it is a false one. People may well comment, "Oh, that's just the way he is" when they witness the behavior.

Two men were walking through the grounds of a county fair. As the noon hour approached, one man said to the other, "I'll treat you to a hot dog." After a long wait in line, the man came back with two hot dogs and handed one to his friend who had located an empty table in the shade. His friend took the hot dog and stood up, shouting loudly, "You know I never eat relish!" Then he took the hot dog and threw it into his friend's face. He had thrown temper tantrums from the time he was a child, and they had always gotten him what he wanted.

I was reminded of this incident not long ago when I was eating in a restaurant. Suddenly a carton of milk plummeted through the air from behind me and splattered on the floor a few feet away from my table. Turning around, I saw a little boy looking triumphantly at the mess he had caused. His mother looked embarrassed, and his father was mumbling something about leaving the child home next time. The mess was quickly cleaned up by an obliging busboy and the incident was forgotten, even by the parents of the little boy, whose behavior was rewarded by his being given the desired glass of coke, which had precipitated the temper tantrum in the first place. This little boy is well on his way to becoming an adult who throws a tantrum whenever he doesn't get his way. If the tantrums keep getting him what he wants, he may well be on his way toward being a grownup like the man with the hot dog.

Adult temper tantrums are not an uncommon problem to be presented in a counseling office such as mine. Indeed, the problem seems on the increase. Coffee thrown across the breakfast table, valuable papers cut in shreds, good china broken into bits, a model plane or a piece of sculpture dashed against a wall—all of these are ways in which many people react when something displeases them. There is no major difference between these examples or the one of the man and the hot dog or the little boy throwing his milk in a restaurant. All are examples of temper tantrums, except that in the example of the milk the person was only about two years old.

Temper tantrums at any age are simply ways to get what a person wants. If they work at two, they may well be repeated at twenty—or fifty! By that time they have become an old tape, a very destructive tape. When a child lies down in the middle of the supermarket and screams because his mother will not buy him candy, the easiest way to quiet him is to buy him the candy he desires. The result is instant peace. But the lifelong result is a person who in childhood discovered that temper tantrums work, and so those tantrums become an old tape, played often in order to get whatever he or she wants.

For though it is hard to literally walk away from a child who is screaming on the floor, to let a child develop a pattern of temper tantrums is not a kindness to the child. If the incident occurs in public, it is embarrassing for the parent, and the natural reaction will be to try to stop the obnoxious behavior by almost any means possible. But to buy the child the candy he is screaming for is to establish a lifelong pattern of destructive tapes which will be harder to cut as an adult.

For temper tantrums are not restricted to the very young only. Adults, too, are capable of having them. People may give in to an adult temper tantrum for the moment to avoid the same embarrassment and general discomfort which are created by childhood tantrums. But ultimately the world will not put up with such behavior in adults.

A woman came into my office wondering why her husband had suddenly left her. When I questioned her further, she said that they had been arguing right before he left and she had ended up the fight by breaking his eyeglasses. Apparently such behavior was not an unusual ending for their arguments, and so her question was, "Why now?"

My best guess was that the husband had probably gotten tired of broken glasses and had decided not to let it happen again. His lack of warning to her about his leaving was obvious. He didn't want another temper tantrum and so, as she put it, "He sneaked out."

In the same way, a multitude of negative tapes relating to behavior and attitudes become stored up in our lives. A certain behavior works, or we get by with it, and so we continue it. Some people automatically cheat whenever it seems to be to their advantage. Others are consistently defeated when anything goes wrong with their plans, rather than looking for alternate ways. Some develop sloppy work habits, such as letting dishes pile up or neglecting to open bills. Some never return phone calls or they assume that anyone who disagrees with them must not like them. Alcoholism, drug abuse, overeating, nail-biting are all, to a lesser or greater degree, old tapes. The list is endless. And to the person involved, it feels as though they are bound to the behavior; they cannot change. That is the way they are!

Some negative tapes come also in the shape of "what ifs" and "why nots." Sometimes these tapes relate to trivial, but nevertheless annoying, aspects of life. A while back a friend spent the night in my guest room and brought her small cocker spaniel puppy. When I went to bed, I took my own older dog into my bedroom. This was too much for the cocker, who decided around midnight that he wanted to get out of the guest room and play with my dog. For hours, it seemed, he sat by the guest room door, scratching and occasionally barking. Then the sounds died down.

Now I can sleep, I thought. But then, as I almost drifted into sleep, a thought struck me: *What if he barks again?* It was like waiting for the proverbial shoe to drop. It was a tape. And I was wide awake again. Only when I realized that this was just an old tape of "what if" was I able to cut the tape and focus away from it. After that, sleep came quickly.

Sometimes, however, the "what ifs" are much more threatening than the missing of one night's sleep. "What if I had come home early the night that Johnny ran away?" "Why can't we be rich like everyone else?" "Why did the business deal fall through?" "Why can't I look like the girl next door?" "Why don't my children ever visit me?" "What if I lose my job?" And so one could go on with a myriad of possibilities of "what ifs" and "why nots." They are innumerable. And each of us has our own personal favorites.

The problem with such a line of thinking is that it leads to a dark, gloomy pit which is the opposite of a safety zone. One is reminded of the childhood stories of Winnie-the-Pooh, and especially of the old grey donkey, Eeyore, who lived in a very gloomy place. Eeyore could always be counted on to see the bad side as he

> stood by himself in a thistly corner of the forest, his front feet well apart, his head on one side, and thought about things. Sometimes he thought sadly to himself, "Why?" and sometimes he thought, "Wherefore?" and sometimes he thought, "Inasmuch as which?"—and sometimes he didn't quite know what he *was* thinking about. So when Winnie-the-Pooh came stumping along, Eeyore was very glad to be able to stop thinking for a little, in order to say "How do you do?" in a gloomy manner to him.[1]

For anything can become a tape. Tapes that are safety zones are positive, happy memories, or dreams of what might be, or a sense of satisfaction from having done our best. They remind us that there have been happy times in the past and that there can be fulfillment in the future. These tapes sustain and encourage us to go on.

Negative tapes do quite the opposite. They discourage us about the past and assure us that there is no hope in the future. As we play these tapes, they take over and become pervasive in our lives. We get frantic. And if we don't stop at some point, the tapes begin to seem as if they will play forever.

In the case of going through our monthly bills, for example, we say: "I can't do them; I just don't feel like it." Then we cop out with, "That is just the way I am," and we feel trapped by what we feel is our inescapable temperament. Depending on the nature and intensity of the tapes, we may feel as though we will never be free of the past nor successful in the future. And at the extreme, reaching the point of desperation, the situation may become so futile and hopeless that the tapes may overwhelm and suicide may feel like the only way out.

In her book, *Beyond Ourselves,* Catherine Marshall relates,

> When I lived in the nation's capital, I used to notice how often the Washington papers reported suicide leaps from the Calvert Street Bridge over Rock Creek Park. In fact, this happens so repeatedly that the site is often called "suicide bridge."
>
> It was easy to sense the human tragedy behind these brief notices—the plunge of the young wife of an Air Force major who learned that she had an inoperable cancer, or that of the elderly man whose wife had just died. These were people in the grip of circumstances which they felt helpless to change. They saw no way out of their predicaments except the way that lay over the bridge.[2]

They played the tapes of "what if" and "why not" until the tapes tangled up with no way out except by smashing the machine. In these cases, real tragedy may well have become escalated rather than subdued by the playing of negative tapes, by "talking it out" and "working through it." For at this point of desperation, effective counseling is that which objectifies the situation and helps the person to turn away from the negative thinking rather than pushing him or her further into it.

Recently, as I was staying by the ocean for a few days, I noticed greater extremes in high and low tides than I have ever seen before. The waves would appear so high and threatening that it was hard to envision a low tide. Yet within a relatively short time the sea was calm and the tide had gone out the distance of a city block or more.

One afternoon, as I stood on rocks which shortly before had been underwater, I was impressed as never before with the certainty that the tide truly does always come in and always go out. The analogy between the tide and the changing circumstances of our lives is not a new one, but for me that day it was very new. Life will always have its tragedies as well as its trivial annoyances. Life, too, will have its ecstasies and its simple pleasures. Neither the good nor the bad can be eradicated. It is not possible for any of us to eliminate negative experiences from our lives, for there are times when life overwhelms each of us and the negative tapes are triggered. Then we retreat like scared children to whatever refuge we can find. We need our safety zones.

But my teenage friend who lost her father was right. Ultimately we do retain the basic control over our emotions. The tapes can be cut. We can refocus. We cannot stop many of the blows with which life strikes us nor our immediate reactions to those blows. But we can control our attitude toward our suffering, and thus we can often determine how long this suffering lasts. Negative tapes may *feel* permanent, but they do not have to be.

A teenager sought my professional help after her mother died from cancer. Karen had stayed away from school for over a month since her mother's death, and she saw no way to end the depression which she felt. By the time I saw her, she was playing tapes on top of tapes.

Not only was Karen just plain depressed about her mother's death, she also had temporarily destroyed even the good memories of the past by playing the tapes of those memories way past the good of a safety zone, to the point where they tortured her because the happy times could never be repeated. Then she tormented herself with the "what ifs" of the bad times: "If I had only done more around the house when she was sick," or "If I had only stayed with her the night she died instead of running from death like a frightened child." She worried about her grades at school, her family's finances, her father's health, and even had herself convinced that cancer ran in the family and that she, too, would get it. The tapes, added to the natural grieving process, had almost incapacitated her for anything else by the time I met her.

After a few counseling sessions in which she learned to cut the tapes and focus her thoughts back to more positive things, such as her present work at school, her many friends, and the hobbies she loved, Karen began to experience less depression. She was able to go back to school and go on with her life. Actually, focusing on school became part of her therapy. As she said later, "I stopped playing the tapes of what had happened and didn't even start looking at the 'what ifs' of the future." As she did this, her self-image became positive once again, for she felt a greater confidence in her ability to handle the future even if it didn't always turn out as she wanted it to.

To cut the tapes and refocus—it all sounds so tantalizingly simple and yet so impossible. Perhaps too simple and therefore impossible. Yet I have seen this to be a liberating factor in people with problems ranging from depression to child abuse and sexual molestation. Once again, sometimes children state issues more simply than we adults who tend to distrust simplicity. As one child said regarding the vicious beatings which had been inflicted on her earlier in her life: "I just don't think about them anymore, and so I'm happy." Harmful repression? I don't think so. Intuitively she has learned to cut tapes.

I don't think I fully understood the power of the human mind to control its own destiny until my mother's death. Nor did I realize the power of positive tapes as safety zones and the equally strong potential for my tapes to destroy me. As I stood in the lobby of a hospital emergency room on a warm August afternoon a few years ago, I felt a nauseating numbness from the blow which had just struck my life. My mother and aunt were both headed for intensive care units after their car accident. These were almost my only living relatives. One by one most of the others had all died in a sort of awesome procession during the same decade. Now, as I faced sudden and complete aloneness from the severing of family ties, the tapes played. I remember thinking, "This is what you read about in the paper from time to time and you thank God it's not happening to you. But now it is happening to you. . . ." I resolved at that moment that, while I would certainly never be the same again, neither would I let this tragedy destroy me. I would grow through it; I would indeed use it to grow personally and to understand and help other people more deeply. I made a choice regarding my emotions.

A few days later, as I stood in the doorway of my mother's hospital room just an hour after her death, I overheard a nurse say: "I thought for sure the aunt would die tonight, not the mother." Again I had that unreal feeling of "not me." For I was barely handling my mother's death and it hadn't even occurred to me that my Aunt Lydia might die the same night.

Again, with an act of the will, I made a choice regarding my emotions. I decided that both deaths were more than I could take that night, and so I would simply handle the death that was at hand. Hopefully that would be all that was necessary. I could not emotionally afford to play the tapes of "what if."

In everyday life, however, most of us are more often confronted with tapes of daily living than we are with tapes of great tragedy or enormous danger. A piece of gossip, a delayed promotion, a difficult child, or just a difficult day—these make up part of the fabric of everyday life. It is as we cut negative tapes in these areas and then press on to more positive things that we not only improve the quality of our everyday lives, but also establish positive ways of dealing with tapes which can help us immensely when major tragedies do occur.

Sometimes tapes are triggered by seemingly obscure events. During my mother's accident, death and burial, I held together pretty well. Then one day as I was going through her things I came across an old garden glove which she must have taken off and tucked under a flower-pot by the back door. The tapes flooded my mind: her rose garden in full bloom, the fruit trees which my father had cultivated so carefully and she had continued to care for. Once again I could imagine my mother digging happily in the garden with those old gardening gloves and her floppy straw hat.

Feelings came, too, along with the memories—feelings which had been suppressed for too long and needed to be let out. I remembered reading in a book by Madeleine L'Engle about the good cry she was going to have after her mother died and never had because it was never the right time. It had never been the right time for me, either. But now I had my cry.

Then it was time to cut the tapes and refocus, for what was for the moment a healthy release of emotion could have easily become an old, negative tape which could have made my mother's death seem new again, as if it had just happened. It was bad enough to have her die once. I didn't need to experience losing her over and over.

For negative tapes are brought out by the same kind of things which precipitate positive tapes. A line of music can remind us of a wonderful time in the past or it can stab us with painful memories of a separation from someone we once loved deeply. Once these tapes are playing in full force, the effect can be devastating, for it becomes as if it were happening all over again. When one is dealing with painful memories, for example, the temptation is to doubt that we ever recovered from the event in the first place.

In her play, *Go Back for Murder*, Agatha Christie tells the story of a young woman who was adopted as a child and then much later found out that her natural mother had been convicted of killing her natural father. In a sequence of events designed to confirm or disprove the validity of that conviction, the scene is reenacted by the original participants of that fateful day, with the exception of the natural mother, who had died in prison. After some considerable role-playing, one character exclaims, "It's brought it all back—just as though it happened yesterday."[3]

"Just as though it happened yesterday:" that is the practical essence of what occurs when we play old tapes. It is as though it never stopped happening.

Sometimes the connection between what triggers our tapes and the reality of the situation is very slim indeed. A woman whom I see at infrequent intervals came into my office utterly frantic over the marriage problems of her best friend's daughter. I couldn't understand why she was so upset until she gave me the clue. She explained that her own ten-year-old daughter had a similar personality to that of the friend's daughter. "What if Susan grows up to have the same problems?" she asked desperately, with that frantic sound in her voice which is so characteristic of all of us when we are playing negative tapes. In this case, the lady had gone from someone else's marital problems to those which might be faced by her own daughter—who at this time was still into Cabbage Patch® dolls and dollhouses!

I have learned, too, that sometimes when people talk to me about a problem of the present they are drawing heavily on tapes of the past. What happened long ago heightens their feelings about what is occurring in their lives now. We all do this to some degree, although we do not always recognize what we are doing.

My then eighty-four-year-old Aunt Lydia did survive the accident which killed my mother. Three years later, she fell and broke her hip for the third time. For me, it was emergency rooms, surgery, and interminable waiting all over again. But whereas before I had been relatively calm and in control, this time I fidgeted, fussed, and finally became highly anxious. I had lost my touch, I thought. I couldn't handle these things anymore.

I finally realized that I wasn't just enduring my aunt's hip surgery; I was playing tapes of my mother's death and the illnesses and deaths of all the other relatives before her. When I realized this, I forcibly stopped my thoughts from wandering back to those other times, and also I tried to do something diverting, such as going out for dinner with a friend, on days when I spent more time than usual at the hospital. Thus I could more easily refocus my thinking away from all those past tapes which were sitting there at the surface of my memory, waiting to be played. Such breaks were safety zones which helped me to refocus after cutting the negative tapes.

Safety zones can be an important help in focusing away from negative tapes. Yet, conversely a safety zone can lose its ability as a refuge because of old tapes. Someone whom I had seen in my office for a while was feeling overwhelmed by her job. She needed safety zones. One which seemed ideal was found by converting an extra bedroom into a den with a television set, stereo, and other physical items conducive to relaxation. After several weeks, when her anxiety level was still high in spite of her newly created hideout, I suddenly realized what had happened. To start with, she had connected a phone from her work to her house, so that she wouldn't miss any calls! That, combined with the fact that she never cut off mentally from her work during the day, was enough to make the new room ineffective as a safety zone. Her safety zone ceased to be a safety zone because she brought her negative tapes into it.

Working in the same room where one sleeps, eating heavy meals during the tension of a business meeting, allowing phones to control one rather than making them a useful tool—all of these are the kind of habits which militate against the effective use of safety zones. To the contrary, they feed the unrest and panic of old, negative tapes.

No tape is ever eradicated, even though we may have consciously forgotten it and feel that we've finally gotten through a situation. It has been forty some years now since the Allied Forces liberated one of Hitler's most atrocious death camps, Auschwitz. Going back to the camp forty years later, a former inmate was quoted by a Los Angeles

Times article as saying, "I thought that all my experiences had been erased from my mind, but it wasn't true. I developed two ulcers and had to seek psychiatric help . . ."

Each of us carries around permanent tapes of our past experiences, both good and bad. We can choose to play those tapes or not. But what is most certain about them is that they do not erase. Like the woman at Auschwitz, we may feel that we are finally rid of them. Then something happens which jars the memory, and the feelings and thoughts all come back as if they had never left.

None of us ever knows the real meaning of freedom until we choose to control our old tapes rather than allowing those tapes to control us. We can choose to play positive tapes, using them as a safety zone, and we can decide when to cut them before they turn into negative tapes. We can cut negative tapes as they start, and by so doing we will have decided against living through the pain of a situation over and over again. We have a choice.

Recently I was invited to a birthday dinner which was being given for the mother of two of my childhood friends who used to be my next-door neighbors. The ties between our two families go back a long way. The parents were close friends of my parents, and as children their son and daughter and I constantly played together. For most of our childhood years we grew up together. We shared many vacations, spent time at each other's houses, and were at times as close as any family.

I was excited about the birthday party and felt good about being part of it. Yet it was also hard to see so many faces from the past in one place, while all of my family who knew them so well are gone. It was hard, and yet comforting at the same time.

In this situation, there were two sets of tapes which I could choose to play: "How sad it is that my family is not here to celebrate, too" or "How nice it is that these people are still here for me to associate with all the good memories of the past as well as for me to enjoy in the present."

I had a choice. I could play the positive tapes or the negative ones. This event could be a safety zone in my life now and later in my memories, or it could produce a nightmare of old tapes. I chose the former and had a wonderful time. Of course, the old tapes came to me from time to time, but because I had made a positive choice ahead of time it was relatively easy to cut them and refocus or even to turn negative tapes into positive ones by changing the viewpoint or emphasis.

In an era where Premenstrual Syndrome has been considered a viable defense for murder, it is hard for us to feel that we have any control at all over our emotions. As one teenage boy said to me, "I don't feel like studying, so I can't get good grades." Somehow this "I don't feel like it so I can't" attitude comes off like freedom: "I do my own thing. I do as I feel." But actually it is a very heavy, subtle form of bondage. The English poet who wrote that iron bars do not a prison make was on target, for the greatest human bondage of all can exist within the emotions. The fact that we have more control over these emotions than we imagine can be liberating.

A woman who suffered from much abuse as a child had often attempted suicide as a teenager. Now in her twenties, she stood at the edge of a mountain cliff, once again contemplating the escape of death. Then suddenly she jerked herself back, exclaiming, "This is crazy; it's just a tape. I don't have to do this!" For what had started earlier in her life as a real desire to die had become by now an old tape, an automatic response to stress. As she said later, "In that one moment up there on the mountain I realized for the first time that I could control that emotion instead of its controlling me." That indeed is the freedom of choosing to control ones tapes.

The Safety Zone
Of Balance

I'm pregnant and I'm engaged to be married, but the father of my baby is my fiancé's best friend," exclaimed a young woman in her late twenties. She threw the statement at me as if to say, "There it is! Now, either help me or reject me and get it over with."

Sandra was a slightly built, fragile-looking woman with a fierce gleam of determination in her eyes which more than compensated for that first impression she gave of vulnerability. As she began to tell her story, she vacillated between tears of helplessness and fear and verbalizations of intense anger and bitterness.

The child of missionary parents, Sandra had spent her early years abroad. In those days, she was expected to be the perfect missionary child, an example to others. Yet, except for being trained in manners and routine Bible doctrine, she was largely neglected and unnurtured as a child, with most of the practical aspects of her upbringing left to a live-in nanny. For the most part, there was no one to answer even her simplest questions. When she did ask questions about God, she was punished for "having such doubts." She was afraid to ask about sex, especially as she grew older and heard muffled protests and other sounds she did not understand emanating from her parents' room at night. When she finally grew old enough to dare to ask questions about sex and sexual morality, she no longer had questions. She had found her own way in life and would have resented anything her parents might have said.

In her teenage years, Sandra lived in strictly run boarding schools, where God continued to be portrayed as a hard, unloving Taskmaster who was against all forms of fun and who had deprived her of even her parents when she was a small child and needed them. She had come to hate her parents, foreign missions in general, and above all God—if, as she put it, "He ever existed at all." By adulthood, in rebellion against her background, she had thrown out all of her past, the good along with the bad, and plunged headlong into a promising career where she made good money and led a fast social life.

Now Sandra's ride in the fast lane, so to speak, had been halted abruptly with this unwanted pregnancy and the fear that her fiancé would find out that she had been sleeping with his best friend. Sandra had avoided the extremes of her parents' lives by going to the opposite extreme. And by so doing she had put herself into deeper bondage than ever, even though for a long time her new lifestyle had seemed to offer her freedom.

That day in my office she was like a small child again, this time reaching out, wishing for answers, yet still skeptical of finding any. She had been wounded by the extremes of her parents and then again by her own excesses. Neither extreme had satisfied. Yet I suppose that the tight rigidity of her parents' beliefs had provided a place which, to them, had seemed like a safety zone. Likewise, Sandra had chosen an extreme which she viewed as liberty, which then became for her a sort of safety zone of protection from the opposite extremes of her childhood. To both Sandra and her parents, these extremes felt like safety zones, and in a very limited way they served for a while in that capacity.

For not everything that looks like a safety zone is healthy. Even alcoholism or drug addiction can feel like a safety zone at times; both numb the senses and provide a temporary, false sense of security. But such false safety zones just feel as though they are safe until something shows them to be the opposite. While imbalance may, at times, feel like a safety zone because it's easy to cling to and does not require the effort of balance, only in certain, unique situations does extremism provide a real safety zone.

Yet because of their simplicity the false security of extremes can be appealing. I'm sure that the people who took cyanide at the command of their cult leader in Jonestown, Guyana, a few years ago thought that they had found a safety zone—total care, communal living, so-called spiritual challenge. But Jonestown was a façade, and death by cyanide was the real gauge of its level of safety. It was like a storefront in an old western, looking so authentic and substantial to those who believed in it, while all the time it had no substance at all and could only, in the end, crash. For false safety zones of extremism do not have the firm foundations of real safety zones. They do not have balance. They are not true safety zones.

Back in the late sixties, when I was teaching school, we as a nation became very identity-oriented. "Know thyself" became the popular slogan, and most people who spouted the words genuinely believed that the concept was brand-new instead of just newly rediscovered or new to them. The idea of setting personal goals became somewhat passé, along with the flag, national pride, and the idea of making money.

In more recent years, as the pendulum began to swing back toward the middle, it was a relief to see at least a modicum of national pride, along with a desire for personal achievement, creep slowly back into our culture. For me it was perhaps not until the 1984 Olympics in Los Angeles, as I watched that tremendous outpouring of nationalism and became once again a part of a nation whose people felt a thrill of ecstasy each time the national anthem was played, that I realized we had once again come full circle. American flags were back, to wave and to display rather than to burn or stamp into the mud. Gradually, too, I realized that we were moving back to a greater emphasis on goals and success, even though I might not always agree with the specific definition which was placed on success.

When I was a student, history teachers had talked about these pendulum swings in man's history—how man always seems to avoid one extreme by going to the other. The indulgences and the opulent living of one generation, for example, seems to lead into a spartan austerity in the next generation. Again, these extremes feel like safety zones because each extreme is a drastic attempt to avoid the previous, opposite extreme which has shown itself to be undesirable.

In this way, man has always appeared to have a built-in incapacity for balance. For example, communism is avoided in a Nazi Germany by the fascism of an Adolf Hitler; and then, when the extremes of both forms of total-itarianism seem no different from each other in terms of degrees of evil, we are surprised.

On a nonpolitical level, people who were raised on the theory of letting a child express himself freely often raise their own children with a good deal of suppression and discipline. Very rarely do you see a country or an individual who takes the best from two extremes, drops the radical parts, and comes out with a rational blending of the two. So many youngsters in the sixties who flaunted the material success of their parents, at the same time they lived off of it, are now frequently to be found as corporate executives, struggling with more determination than even their parents to get to the top. Rather than enriching their materialistic drives by some of that idealism from the sixties, they have dropped the one for the other.

In a world which seems to be changing more rapidly each day, the use of simple yet sound safety zones fosters a sense of balance. As I was growing up, one of my heroes was General Douglas MacArthur. I even wrote to him once, and one of the thrills of my preadolescent days was when he actually wrote back! As an adult I felt compelled a number of years later to learn about this man for myself rather than depending on what I had been told about him when I was a child. One aspect of his life that struck me deeply was the level of balance which he exhibited in his private life. His was a balance which was maintained partly through the use of safety zones, a balance which enabled him to live through times of great stress when he was what has been called by many: America's greatest soldier.

In my opinion, one of the most magnificent achievements of MacArthur's career lay in his dealing with the Japanese people when, after conquering that nation, he became head of the occupation forces. The Japanese people expected revenge and pillage from such a conqueror; instead, they came to worship him as they had once worshiped their Emperor. He understood the Japanese mind, and from that understanding grew a compassionate yet firm rebuilding of a wartorn nation.

In this task he was virtually alone, and the pressures were great. Yet as in earlier years, when as Supreme Commander in the Pacific he had fought the war which all but leveled Japan, now in rebuilding what he had once torn down he innately developed a network of safety zones which preserved a sense of balance in his personal life. In a typical day in Japan, MacArthur established a structure which balanced out his work schedule. Regular exercise in the morning and a routine nap in the afternoon; time with his young son, Arthur, and with his favorite cocker spaniel dog; regularly scheduled movies in the evening during six days out of the weeks—these were some of his safety zones. Others ranged from a devoted wife and a close and long-time aide, Col. Sid Huff, with whom he could ventilate his feelings, to a special old wicker rocking chair, which had been painted red and was kept in his bedroom but was brought down every night when MacArthur watched his movie. Explains Sid Huff in his book, *My Fifteen Years with General MacArthur*:

Just where it [the chair] had come from nobody seemed to know, but the General had it with him in the Southwest Pacific and later in Manila, and he ordered it brought on to Tokyo. There was a cushion in the seat of the chair and the back was just the right height to meet the back of his head when he settled down, stretched out his long legs and leaned far back to look up at the movie screen. You could see him relaxing as he lit his cigar and puffed away.[1]

All of these were simple but effective safety zones which balanced MacArthur's life in the middle of demands which could have thrown the most balanced life into chaos. Some close companions, a little structure, an old chair, a movie, and a cigar or his famous corncob pipe—all so very simple, yet so very vital to a life of balance and productivity.

Structure and the use of movies shown after dinner were also safety zones for Winston Churchill during his time as Prime Minister of England during World War II. Says a Churchill bodyguard assigned by Scotland Yard:

Churchill's week-ends at Chequers during the war were alike as two peas. Our Friday arrivals, usually about four, were like small invasions of the house. . . . Mr. Churchill, upon arrival, would always first of all have his bath. He was as insistent about this as the famous tenor Caruso was reputed to have been. . . . Bathed and refreshed, he would climb into his half comical and thoroughly practical siren suit. He wore this to dinner. He did not care what anyone else wore either and his dinner table was usually the ultimate in incongruity of apparel. After dinner he would retire for a moment, then come back dressed in one of his gorgeous oriental dressing gowns. He always wore one of these during the film showings, which were his passion. After the showing, he would chat briefly with his guests, then go to work. . . . Usually he worked till three a.m., often till four, sometimes clear through the night.

The cinema gave Mr. Churchill a sort of mental liberation, and seemingly the noisier and busier the story and the more oppressing its plot, the more it relaxed his mind.

Films seemed to focus his eye and to engage the surface apparatus of his mind, while the deeper thinking that he had to do by himself went on inside. His mind lived on these two levels.[2]

It is interesting to me that these two men, who were two of the most pivotal figures during World War II, had these similarities in their use of safety zones. Structure and diversion seemed to be the key to the survival of both. These safety zones balanced out the extreme tensions in their lives. It is even more intriguing to speculate on the success of the war and the fate of the entire world as we know it had these men been foolish enough to try to survive without safety zones.

Yet if safety zones provide balance to our lives, an attitude of balance can in itself become a major safety zone. To avoid being caught up in the extremes of the monumental changes which are occurring around us, we do indeed need the safety zone of balance. In my own lifetime, for example, we have moved from an assumption that marriage and children were a woman's only option to an orientation toward the development of a career above all else—and now back to an almost frantic need to have it all, family and career. All of these positions are extremes, and each in its own way leads to a frustrated existence.

In the Bible we are presented with a more balanced picture of womanhood: Deborah, a judge and married; Lydia, a business woman; Priscilla, married and yet a teacher of the Church; and Lois, who was faithful in the raising of her children and grandchildren are just a few examples. All of these women seemed to be women of balance. They each had an individual focus, and they did not seem to live frustrated lives of trying to fulfill too many roles. Even though we do not have many details about their lives, it seems apparent that at times they felt led to differing priorities. We think of Deborah and her skill at battle, even though she was married. We know that Lois greatly influenced Timothy, even though she undoubtedly did many other things with her life. They seemed to be a group of women who fit into God's particular plan for their lives, a plan which varied from woman to woman.

Today, too, marriage, children, and a career are all possibilities for any woman. To have an attitude of balance is to acknowledge that what might be right for one woman might not be right for another. Furthermore, that which is right for a woman at one period in her life might change at a later time. Above all, to have an attitude of balance is to acknowledge that it is impossible to do it all. Such an attitude is a safety zone, for it keeps one's life within sound perimeters and helps avoid the futility of trying to walk on water.

About five years ago, I came very close to adopting a child. My desire to do so was very deep, and my choice not to do so came at great personal cost. Yet for me at that time, adoption was not right. I knew that I could not have a full-time counseling practice, continue my writing career, and be a parent all at one time without neglect in at least one of those areas. Since I would not have neglected the child or the practice, I knew that my writing would probably be the area which would suffer. In a sense, then, I chose my writing over adoption. It almost sounds cold when I write the words, but I am convinced God has led me to write, and I do not dare disregard that guidance, nor do I want to.

It was hard to choose against adoption, but to live a life of trying to do it all would have been even harder and would have also hurt other people whom I would have had to neglect—including, perhaps, my own child. Some day my priorities may change, or they may change temporarily, but for now the pathway I have chosen is right for me. I can only do so much, and so I must choose the path which God had laid out for me at this time. That belief is a safety zone for me. For it rises above what the current fad is or what others think I should do or even what everyone else is doing. It is the safety zone of the balance of the will of God.

There is something about us human beings which is attracted to imbalance. Sometimes it just seems glamorous, and when the extremism is in the area of burnout, the resultant fatigue brings sympathy from others who tell us what we want to hear—"that we work too hard." There seems to be a tinge of nobility in going all out rather than going along, unglamorously, at a balanced speed toward realistic goals.

This is not to say that imbalance is never used of God. At times a person may be led to go at a faster speed than is normally wise, or someone may be forced to take a stand of extremism in order to be true to his or her conscience. During World War II, this was certainly true of a woman like Corrie Ten Boom as she saved Jews in Holland. Or the Swedish diplomat, Raoul Wallenberg, as he fought night and day against impossible odds to save one hundred thousand Jews in Hungary.

But imbalance is not, in general, a good principle of life. To the contrary, moderation is strongly emphasized in the Bible both by example and precept. Christ Himself is our greatest example. When He owed taxes to the government, He paid them. When He was weary, He left crowds of needy people in order to refurbish Himself for further service. When He was angry over the abuses in the temple, He expressed that anger vividly, and yet His rage did not possess Him permanently. His sacrifice on the cross was an example of divine extremism, one of those exceptions we talked about; but in His daily life, Jesus Christ exemplified the use of the safety zone of balance.

In an age where we have a hard time even defining life and death itself, the organized Christian world, along with everyone else, seems to vacillate from extreme to extreme. Yet we have always tended toward imbalance, even when we lived in simpler times. Years ago, when the airplane first came into being, certain Christians actually thought flying was a sin. Since we didn't have wings, God obviously didn't mean for us to fly, they reasoned. Yet today God's Word is introduced into certain remote areas of the world only because of the miracle of air travel.

On a different level, when I was a child I was forbidden to attend the theater. When I asked why, I was told that the movies were not uplifting spiritually. I could understand that, as a general principle. But when I brought up movies such as the older Disney films and nature stories, my undaunted parents then said that the theater was wrong because of the people you mingled with. To go to the theater was to become too much a part of their world. When I then replied that I didn't see much difference between the people who went to the theater and the people who rode on a bus, they didn't know what to say.

My parents finally had enough honesty to admit that I had a point and that for me to go to some of the better movies was not a sin. But many people in the organized church still resist such balance. Because some movies are negative in their impact, they indict the whole movie industry. Yet, ironically, many of these same people watch all kinds of junk on the television screen in their own living rooms. That, too, is imbalance.

As one young man said to me regarding the general imbalance of the organized Christian church: "It used to confuse me to go to Sunday school and sing, 'Jesus loves the little children, all the children of the world,' and then go home and hear my aunt, who was the Sunday school teacher, talk about how afraid she was that 'niggers' would move into our neighborhood."

At the other extreme, however, we have Christians who, in the name of so-called Christian liberty and some brand of pseudo-intellectualism, combine "doing your own thing" and irreverently calling upon the "Man Upstairs" for help, as though God were some kind of cosmic pal dispensing giant aspirin pills to instantly meet our finite whims.

As an example of Christian balance, freedom to go to

the movies does not mean that it is right to watch every movie around, including those which feed into our homes day after day through our television sets. The choice of each movie we see, or don't see, is in itself a decision which must be made in balance.

Sometimes I think we are so afraid of so-called "situation ethics" and just plain gray areas—as opposed to everything being either black or white—that we lock ourselves into a mindset which declares that everything must be right or wrong, bad or good, never in-between.

At the risk of oversimplification, "situation ethics" is a value system which takes love as the sole determiner of the right and wrong of behavior. To include love as a *part* of the motivation of one's behavior, a single factor among others in determining the morality of that behavior, is certainly biblical. God Himself delayed His destruction of the city of Sodom because of His love and respect for Abraham, who kept pleading with God to wait. Yet, eventually, love was not enough; for God's righteousness demanded that Sodom be destroyed.

For love alone is not enough of a basis for determining morality. Yet it is neither balanced nor scriptural to avoid the extremes of "situation ethics" by going to the other extreme of throwing out love. Nor is it possible in any practical sense of the word to say that ethical decisions are always made by the application of biblical teaching without any interpretation of the teaching relative to the specific situation at hand.

It is clear biblical teaching that the Scriptures as we have them are the literal Word of God and are to be treated as such. Yet not every issue we encounter is dealt with specifically in the Bible, and for these issues we can only take certain principles which are laid down in the Scriptures and apply them.

There are no verses, for instance, that prescribe the appropriate use of respirators or dialysis machines or mechanical hearts. There are no specific statements about what to do with frozen fetuses, no specific guidelines about the morality of certain ways of producing a human being. As modern technology continues to rush ahead with a speed beyond our natural coping ability, we can no longer afford the self-indulgence of living with simple black-and-white answers. Indeed, we could never afford it, for we have always needed the safety zone of balance.

Thus, whether we like it or not, we must make a choice to either hide our heads and never face the real world in which we live or to take the balance of scriptural precept, under the leading of the Holy Spirit, and make honest decisions regarding these issues which now confront us. For it is only by using the safety zone of balance that we can ever achieve sanity in a world which is changing so fast that without balance we would be jerked back and forth from one extreme opinion to the other.

As a practical example, one could take the problem of the potential annihilation of the Jews during World War II. Some forty years ago, my childhood friends and I celebrated in the streets, banging pots and pans, marking along with the rest of the world the ending of that great conflict. I didn't know a lot then about what was really over, but I knew that something terrible had ended.

From a child's vantage point, the day marked the end of sugar rationing, blackouts and air raid sirens, visiting Japanese friends in American internment camps, and above all seeing horrible war pictures of people being shot and others being stacked and bulldozed into huge piles inside Hitler's death camps. Even then I knew it was time to stop war and make peace. Now I could forget.

But I have not forgotten. I have not been able to forget. I have read books. I have developed friendships with wonderful people who survived the Nazi concentration camps. Those childhood memories of dead, gaunt bodies, stacked and bulldozed in front of my eyes on the movie screen, have taken life. They could have been my friends. They could have been me. They could have been any of us.

The atrocities were carried out by Hitler's special army of hit men, the SS, who were declared at the Nuremberg trials to be a criminal group. They were Hitler's elite, and their vicious deeds were frequently executed with the perverted enjoyment of a sadistic mind.

In the Holocaust, the people one would hope to meet only in a nightmare abounded. And yet they were men, not fictitious monsters from some Gothic horror story. Six million Jews died in the camps, just because they were Jews. Four million others died for helping them or for being in some way disapproved of by the Nazis.

A very dear friend of mine is a survivor of the Bergen-Belsen concentration camp, the camp which surprised the world with its horror on 15 April 1945, when the British entered the camp and found ten thousand unburied bodies. A few days later, the official British gazette in the occupied zone called it "that greatest of all exhibitions of 'man's inhumanity to man.'"[3]

In a sermon at Oxford, C. S. Lewis once said: "There are no ordinary people." He then further explained that we live in a society of "possible gods and goddesses," a society where any person we talk to may some day "be a creature which . . . you would be strongly tempted to worship or else a horror and a corruption such as you now meet, if at all, only in a nightmare." In addition to its men of corruption, the Holocaust had its "gods and goddesses," too: men and women who went to their deaths with a prayer on their lips, people who gave their last crust of bread to one who needed it more, people who risked or even gave their lives to try to save the lives of the Jews around them.

In thinking about that statement of Lewis and relating it to the Holocaust, it has been fruitful for me to ponder the possibilities of my responsibility had I been old enough and in the right place to be confronted with the question of how much to sacrifice to save the lives of others. Would I have had the courage to put into action the convictions which I so easily set down on paper?

Along with the question of how much courage I would have had, there has also been the dilemma of what would have been correct behavior under those circumstances. The Bible clearly states that honesty is a principle of Christian living. But if one compares scripture with scripture, there are some striking illustrations of God's approval of at least some level of deception in certain special incidents.

In Joshua 2, for example, two Israelites were sent into Jericho to spy out the land and city. When the king of Jericho set out to find these spies, a prostitute named Rahab hid them from the king. When she was questioned by the king's men, she said, "There came men unto me, but I [knew] not whence they were: . . . whither the men went, I [know] not: pursue after them quickly; for ye shall overtake them" (vv. 4–5). Rahab was later rewarded for hiding the spies, and her whole family was spared when Jericho was taken. The fact that some level of deceit was both necessary and right in this instance seems apparent by the circumstances and by the response of the spies, as well as by God's ultimate approval of what Rahab did.

Furthermore, in verse 14, when Rahab asked for the lives of her family to be spared, the spies said to Rahab: "Our life for yours, if ye utter not this our business." Since she had already been rather specifically questioned regarding the spies, again it seems fairly certain that she could not have kept her secret without practicing deceit.

Other biblical examples seem to illustrate God's use of deceit in special circumstances. When it was time for Israel to have a new king, "the Lord said unto Samuel, How long wilt thou mourn for Saul, seeing I have rejected him from reigning over Israel?" God then commanded Samuel to go to Jesse, the Bethlehemite, to get a king from among his sons.

Samuel's reply was, "How can I go? If Saul hear it, he will kill me. And the Lord said, Take a heifer with thee, and say, I am come to sacrifice to the Lord. And call Jesse to the sacrifice, and I will show thee what thou shalt do:

and thou shalt anoint unto me him whom I name unto thee. And Samuel did that which the Lord spake" (1 Sam. 16:1–4).

To illustrate once again, in the beginning of Exodus, when the king of Egypt told the midwives to kill every boy-child delivered of a Hebrew woman, the midwives disobeyed that order. Later, when they were questioned about the large numbers of male children who were being born, they replied falsely that, unlike Egyptian women, the Hebrew women tended to have their children before the midwives arrived. We then read that "therefore God dealt well with the midwives: and the people multiplied, and waxed very mighty. And it came to pass, because the midwives feared God, that he [gave them families]" (Exod. 1:20–21).

When people such as Corrie Ten Boom rescued Jews from the clutches of the Nazis, they had to practice a similar deceitfulness if the Jews whom they had hidden were to remain safe. The very presence of the Jews was kept secret by various forms of deception; and anything which could be smuggled in—fake passports, food and forbidden books such as the Bible—were freely used.

In the atmosphere in which we live, terrorism is becoming an international problem of large dimensions. Just a short time ago, when I was writing this chapter, the world heard that the prime minister of Sweden had been assassinated in the streets of Stockholm. One Swedish lady who was interviewed by the press exclaimed, "It's so un-swedish"! Another, similarly reacting to the thought that such an occurrence is not common in Sweden, commented that life would never again be quite the same in Sweden, where a prime minister previously could walk down the streets of his country unguarded and unafraid.

Such an act of terrorism may be un-swedish, but it is very much a part of human nature. And because of the increase of terrorism as a mentality of our times, it is certainly possible that any of us may also be confronted with a moral dilemma where, either to save our own life or the lives of others, we will be asked to deceive those who would do harm.

I would rather face such an issue before it happens, with the quiet leading of the Holy Spirit, than to do as one person suggested when she said: "I would feel that it was always a sin to lie, but if I ever had to face a situation similar to that of Corrie Ten Boom, I would just have to lie and then confess my sin later"!

If one uses balance in scriptural interpretation, I do not believe that one would ever be forced to believe that he or she must sin in order to please God—and then have to turn around and confess that sin! Sin is never the right thing to do! If it is right, it is not sin. If it is sin, then it is not right. Either people like Corrie Ten Boom sinned by their deceit or they greatly glorified God. In my opinion, what Corrie did does not deserve to be desecrated by calling it sin.

It is important, however, to be very careful not to use our God-given freedom in biblical interpretation as a license to sin. If true Christian liberty leads to a freedom to sin, then it is better to stay legalistic in one's thinking. Yet, because it is a scriptural principle that if we truly want God's will and if we are committed to Him He will not fail to guide us, it is not necessary to go to the extreme of legalism to avoid the extreme of abusing our Christian liberty.

Sometimes we are so afraid to trust ourselves and each other that we establish excessively rigid church regulations and set up certain individuals whose word on biblical interpretation becomes tantamount to that of God Himself. God, however, has placed a great deal of faith in the discernment of the individual believer by allowing him or her to interpret His Word, and no amount of church authority can take away that basic God-given right. To do so would be to deny the New Testament teaching of the priesthood of the believer and the authority of the Holy Spirit within.

Balance in Christian thinking and living is not only a safety zone of rational behavior, a way of living which does not go up and down with every new fad of thinking, but such balance also tends to militate against irrational extremism. Balance can actually prevent sin. I have seen leaders in the Christian world who for years are highly legalistic but then suddenly, for no apparent reason, do something really destructive, such as have a sexual affair or steal money from the church. Many times such an abrupt break from all past morality comes from living a long time by such extreme standards that even they cannot keep up with their own legalism. And so they just give up altogether.

In the very contemporary arena of medical ethics I am seeing another area of potential imbalance. People who a few years ago would have fought to keep anyone alive are now coming into my office confused over the escalating ability of medical technology to keep loved ones alive beyond what seems humane. As they realize that the old way of "keep them alive as long as possible" is no longer valid because of its endless potential, many are attempting to compensate by going to an opposite extreme, in which they practically start accepting euthanasia as a viable way of thinking.

The potential of going to one extreme to avoid the other in the area of medical ethics is a frightening one. But the motivation behind most of this thinking is simply not wanting a loved one to suffer. From that point, some people are inclined to go to an extreme based only on what they feel, rather than prayerfully formulating their view of how to handle this new technology according to the safety zone of scriptural principles. For if the older definition of "situation ethics" was based solely on love, a new definition for our age might be based on what we feel. Each is equally dangerous and imbalanced.

An attitude of balance provides a safety zone of consistency. Sometimes we evangelicals are so afraid of the "social gospel," for example, we forget that the same Book which teaches us to confess our sins also teaches us to love our neighbor. *Sin* is a word which belongs in our vocabulary, but so does *love*, along with *self-love* and *self-esteem*.

Not long ago, I listened to an intelligent, highly spiritual man tell me of the evils of a good self-image. Even though he was a man well taught in the Scriptures, he seemed to equate good self-esteem with pride, and self-hate with humility! In his opinion, being spiritual means to dislike oneself. Likewise, he seems to feel that it is sinful to have a positive sense of self-worth.

Self-esteem is the estimate one makes of oneself. A good self-image is based on truth, not a lie. It simply means liking what is good about oneself and finding self-respect in one's attempts to improve those things which one does not like about oneself. In my work as a counselor it is my job, in part, to help people see those things in their lives which can make them feel proud as well as to point out areas which need change. To do this task effectively is to aid in the development of a good self-image.

Kenneth Wuest translates Romans 12:3: "For I am saying through the grace which is given to everyone who is among you, not to be thinking more highly of one's self, beyond that which one ought necessarily to be thinking, but to be thinking with a view to a sensible appraisal (of one's self) according as to each one God divided a measure of faith."

A sensible appraisal, an honest appraisal—that is the meaning of the term *self-esteem*. It does not imply automatic self-hate or self-love. Yet the obvious goal in improving a self-image is to like oneself for what is positive and to change that which is negative so that it, too, can exert a positive affect.

As creatures made in God's image, for the purpose of fellowship with Him, to have self-hate as a goal seems contradictory to any sound psychological or biblical thinking. It seems reasonable to conclude that God is not in the business of making human junk! In the words of psychologist Dr. Rollo May in his book, *Man's Search for Himself*:

> In circles where self-contempt is preached, it is of course never explained why a person should be so ill-mannered and inconsiderate as to force his company on other people if he finds it so dreary and deadening himself. And furthermore the multitude of contradictions are never adequately explained in a doctrine which advises that we should hate the one self, "I," and love all others with the obvious expectation that they will love us, hateful creatures that we are; or that the more we hate ourselves, the more we love God who made the mistake, in an off moment, of creating this contemptible creature, "I."[4]

Again, there is the need for the safety zone of balance when it comes to the issue of self-esteem. The Fall of man is offset by the Atonement of Christ and man's individual acceptance of that atonement. We are born in sin but justified by grace. There is also a need for correct scriptural exegesis. For example, the self referred to in Romans 6 is the old sinful nature which, by the death of Christ, is now to be reckoned dead. It has no direct relationship to the concept of the self which is referred to in the term self-image. They refer to two different things.

We need to be careful, theologically as well as psychologically, in our definition of terms. For just as the term *self-image* refers to the estimate one makes of oneself, *pride* more often than not refers to a *low* self-image, which can then manifest itself in bragging about how great one is.

When I was a teacher in a public high school, for example, one of my colleagues always started the year by telling his students how lucky they were to have him as a teacher. He would then expound upon the many reasons for his superiority: where he attended college, how sophisticated his teaching methods were, and how long his track record was as a teacher. I later found out that this man had always been unpopular as a kid, and that he had come from a family who had no respect for education. I suspect that when he told those students how wonderful he was, he probably was trying to convince *himself* of his worth more than he was trying to convince them.

If much apparent pride is based in low self-esteem, true humility is based in a good self-image. Only if I like myself can I avoid either grabbing for the spotlight or groveling in a murky sort of self-denigration. Both of these are the symptoms of a low self-image. Similarly, to quote Dr. Rollo May once again,

> Much self-condemnation, thus, is a cloak for arrogance. Those who think they overcome pride by condemning themselves could well ponder Spinoza's remark, "One who despises himself is the nearest to a proud man." In ancient Athens when a politician was trying to get the votes of the working class by appearing very humble in a tattered coat with big holes in it, Socrates unmasked his hypocrisy by exclaiming, "Your vanity shows forth from every hole in your coat."[5]

Conceit is the opposite of the comfortable, self-forgetfulness that comes from a good sense of self-worth.

Consistent with this same thought is Amy Carmichael's belief that humility is simply an absence of occupation with one's self. The kind of humility which is upheld in the Scriptures has nothing to do with groveling self-hate. The person who is blessed with a sense of positive self-worth can then go on to do God's work unfettered by the chains of low self-esteem and its resultant self-occupation.

For the practical results of a good self-image are positive, not negative. They are godly, not ungodly. A nurse with a good self-image is able to take on more complicated tasks rather than running away from them out of fear. A student with good self-esteem sets higher career goals for himself because he now believes he can fulfill these goals. A housewife realizes, after a business meeting goes bad and her husband comes home and complains about everything, that it is not she who has caused the problem, and so they are both spared from an argument with each other. A businessman stays with his principles in spite of criticism from colleagues because way down deep within himself he has the courage to believe that he is right. A young delinquent stops vandalizing the neighborhood because he no longer has to prove how tough he is.

It is sometimes necessary to use the tool of psychological counseling in order to achieve a good self-image. Yet I am the first person to admit to the idiocy which is sometimes to be found in the field of psychotherapy. In fact, when I made my decision to be a psychological counselor, I made two conditions before God.

One condition was that God would enable me to cut the tapes of each day's problems, for I knew that had not been one of my strong points even as a teacher. Many times I had worried all night about a student, only to go to school the next day and find that, after my sleepless night of anxiety, the student was now in better shape than I was! The other condition was that God would keep me balanced in a field where I had seen too many Christians begin either to overspiritualize all problems or go to the more dangerous extreme of relegating all problems to psychological solutions with a disregard for and even a denial of God.

Yet psychotherapy itself can be a safety zone of balance. This was confirmed for me by a conversation I heard recently on radio. On this particular show, a man who does a great deal of radio work was answering questions from people who phone in. His discussion had been focused on the evils of psychotherapy. A woman called in who was by this time upset and in tears, not wanting to displease God and yet unwilling to admit that the help which she had received from psychotherapy was evil. After telling of the help which she had received from her therapist and maintaining that her faith had been supported rather than attacked, the woman waited for the man's response. He hesitated, faltered, and then merely reiterated his distrust of psychology.

Finally the woman, by now quite confident and calm, said, "I'm really glad I called you, for now I know that you don't know what you're talking about on this subject. I was right all along, and you were wrong." So ended that segment of the show. I respected the woman's bravery and honesty. She had found a God-given safety zone in psychotherapy, and she had used that safety zone with the tempering of the safety zone of balance.

True balance in the Christian realm is neither wishy-washy nor a sign of compromising one's standards. Actually, to be balanced requires a closer walk with God and a deeper knowledge of His Word than does extremism. It is easy to go to extremes because, for the moment, extremism can feel so safe.

In the area of psychotherapy, for example, it is so easy to label those who seek psychological help as sinful, as not having enough faith in God. It is equally easy to go to the other extreme and feel that all of life's answers are to be found in counseling alone. Neither extreme is accurate. It is sometimes hard to arrive at a place of balance. But the end product of balance is peace with oneself and with God.

For true Christian balance does not change capriciously with the whim of other people's opinions, but rests solidly on the safety zone of the will of God. To have the attitude of balance as a safety zone is comparable to having a rudder on a ship which keeps the ship from going off in the wrong direction and getting lost at sea.

Looking back on my childhood, I realize that my mother was the epitome of balance and that, while I am by nature impulsive and somewhat extreme in my personality, she was the first person who taught me the value of balance. Because of her balance, in a very real sense my mother was the glue which held our family more closely together. This was true of even our extended family. Our house was where most celebrations were held; and whenever there was a squabble anywhere in the family connection, she was the peacemaker.

My mother adored my father, and yet on the morning he died, long after I had grown up, she came back home from the hospital, boiled eggs, made toast, and insisted that we eat. "We have a hard day ahead; we'll need our strength," she said. We could not afford the self-indulgence of being imbalanced and skipping meals. Then, after the funeral arrangements had been made, we went to a special restaurant for lunch. Again, with characteristic balance she felt that if we were to go on we must try to separate ourselves a little from the intensity of the day.

For months after my father's death, my mother spent nights of literal anguish. Yet to all outward appearances she was cheerful. She had to grieve, and yet she also realized that she must not permanently live in that grief, nor did she inflict it upon even us, her children.

A few years later, after my mother died, I remembered more vividly the times in childhood when she had made gloomy days seem cheerful. When I was very small, rainy days always meant something special to do inside, such as new paper dolls or a coloring book. Later, when I was in school, I always knew that on a rainy day I would come home to the smell of cookies baking in the oven. I suppose some of this explains why to this day I love rainy days. Outside the storm may rage, but its contrast to the warmth within makes me feel safe and happy. I don't usually bake cookies on a rainy day, like my mother used to do, but I do often make a pot of homemade soup, which for one night and one day sends a comforting aroma throughout the house.

I remembered, too, that in my childhood my mother had always balanced grief with comfort, pain with joy. This characteristic had not just started with my father's death. To compensate for my childhood illnesses, for example, she used to read me stories which made the afternoon fly, or she would show me how to knit doll clothes out of the scraps of yarn which she had saved in a worn, brocade knitting bag. Sometimes she would just sit and tell me stories of her life as a little girl on a farm in Wisconsin.

Perhaps partly because her sense of balance made her fun as well as encouraging to be with, even in the latter days of her life I truly enjoyed my mother's company. At least once a week we had dinner together, and often friends would join us because they, too, enjoyed those times.

Whatever the specific method used, my mother had learned, long before I knew her, how to balance pain with pleasure. In that way she was my safety zone when I was very young, and then by her example she taught me how I could develop my own safety zone of balance. My pot of soup on rainy days; my dinner out after finishing a chapter of writing; my reading at the end of a day, which transports me away from the frustrations and fatigue of my work—these are some of the simple safety zones in my life which balance me and help me remain productive.

Something simple but satisfying to buffer the cold vicissitudes of life—that is balance. And that balance becomes a safety zone in a world which could otherwise overwhelm us with its fast-paced change.

Chapter
Eight.

Miles to Go Before I Sleep

*I*t was a bright, sunny day at the beach, with just enough crispness in the air to remind me that it was still spring, not summer. The water sparkled in the sunlight, and the sand had that clean, unused, preseason look.

As I settled down on my beach towel and began to absorb the warm rays of the sun overhead, I felt layers of fatigue and tension slowly melt away. The drone of the steady pounding of the waves, punctuated by the occasional cry of a seagull or the shout of a child who, like me, had been drawn to the beach by the feel of the sun rather than the date on the calendar, made me inwardly concur with the poet who wrote that God indeed was in His Heaven and all was right with the world.

This particular beach is a safety zone for me: the same rocky shoreline to which I always retreat and the timeless, blended noises of the sea, the gulls, and the children playing in the same way that they have always played by any ocean in any generation of people.

Still, this year as before it has not been easy to get away, even for just a few days. For whether the safety zone is a weekend by the sea or an evening at home with a good book, life seems to militate against it. Indeed, when the safety zones we seek to use are those which rest both body and mind and prepare us to return refreshed to our task, the demands of unfinished work, the harsh intrusion of the ringing of the telephone, and countless other interruptions will always attempt to prevent us from getting such needed rest.

That great preacher of nineteenth-century England, Charles Haddon Spurgeon, aptly commented on Christ's suggestion to His disciples that they go "apart into a desert place, and rest awhile" (Mark 6:31). Said Spurgeon:

> What? When the people are fainting? When they are like sheep without a shepherd? How can Jesus talk of rest? When the scribes and Pharisees, like wolves, are rending the flock, how can He take His followers on an excursion into a quiet resting place? . . . The Lord Jesus knows better. He will not exhaust the strength of His servants prematurely and quench the light of Israel. Rest time is not waste. It is economy to gather fresh strength. Look at the mower in the summer's day, with so much to cut down ere the sun sets. He pauses in his labor—is he a sluggard? He looks for his stone, and begins to draw it up and down his scythe, with rink-a-tink, rink-a-tink. Is that idle music—is he wasting precious moments? How much might he have mowed while he has been ringing out those notes on his scythe! But he is sharpening his tool, and he will do far more when once again he gives his strength to those sweeps which lay the grass prostrate in rows before him. Nor can the fisherman be always fishing; he must mend his nets. So even our vacation can be one of the duties laid upon us by the kingdom of God.[1]

It is one thing to establish safety zones; it is quite another to use them. Vacation homes are bought and then rarely used; fishing rods lie in closets as new as the day they were purchased; a piece of exercise equipment provides a good decoration for a corner of the basement, but its owner never establishes a routine of exercise. Books lie unread, friendships remain unnurtured, and days off become days to "catch up"—which inevitably seems to mean working harder than ever. In our exhaustion and fatigue the old tapes, which might not even bother us if we were rested, play on unchecked and add to the general fatigue.

Excuses range from a simple "I haven't had time yet" to a more noble sounding "There are just so many needs that I can't turn my back on." The excuses sound noble—noble, that is, until we remember that He who was God Himself made flesh was not beyond the need to turn away from the crowds and refurbish! Such a realization makes our most clever rationalizations of how indispensable we are fade into the ludicrous, if not into rank arrogance.

Once we have established safety zones, it sometimes becomes vital to make them known to others and to use them whether or not others understand. We do not need to persuade, argue, cajole, or even seek approval. We simply need to declare ourselves for ourselves. On one occasion when Christ left the crowds and went with His disciples to the other side of the lake, He went to sleep in the back of the boat. While He slept there arose a great storm which threatened to sink the ship, and the disciples, not understanding how much Christ was still in control of even the wind and the water, criticized Him for not caring. Christ certainly knew this would be their reaction, but He used His safety zones to preserve His human body anyway and did not let the misunderstanding of those around Him dissuade Him.

To declare ourselves for ourselves means to state our own perimeters, our limitations. It is to state that which one needs in order to go on. To declare is to say no to impossible demands. It also means being able to turn down involvement in good causes as well as those which seem to have little value. For anyone can say no to those things which are worthless. But to say no to the demands of the local church or to a missionary cause may be at times exactly what God is asking us to do. For if we do not guard our safety zones we may not have the strength to finish the course which is ahead of us. We will burn out—not for God, but for our own inability to say no.

A young man just out of high school had been involved with drugs but was now well on the path toward making it in his life. A local church group had taken him under their wings, so to speak, while Bill on his own had found a part-time job at a corner drugstore and was starting classes at the nearby junior college. The pastor of the church spent extra time with Bill, shooting baskets in the church gym and in general being available to talk.

As time went on, however, Bill grew increasingly dependent on the pastor. He fell into the habit of turning to the older man several times a day for advice or just for friendship. The pastor let the pattern build until, at the end of his resources and desperate to get his other work done, he began to dodge Bill. He avoided his phone calls and locked himself in his study when he saw Bill approaching. Soon Bill caught on, and, feeling deep rejection, left the church and went back into drugs. The pastor of the small church was never the same again, either. While he blamed himself on the one hand, he also became bitter and angry over his failure to help the young man.

What this pastor failed to see was that he was never meant to do it all. A simple declaration could have solved the whole problem. By declaring his limitations, which had nothing to do with liking or disliking Bill personally, the pastor would have had a good chance at continuing to help Bill. Without that declaration, in the end, Bill interpreted the pastor's actions as rejection rather than realizing that the pastor himself was having difficulty coping. Bill couldn't have been more damaged by the situation than he was, so the pastor's attempts at water-walking didn't do Bill any good anyway. The older man only felt defeated as well as worn out by the experience. Neither profited.

In the long run, to lose one's safety zones in some kind of pseudo-noble effort to walk on water only leads to defeat. We can't walk on water, and sooner or later we all find that out!

To declare oneself does not insure that others will always agree. Here, once again, the safety zone of the will of God becomes vital. If we are doing what he asks of us, what does it matter what others think? Not everyone will agree with us.

150

This has been a hard lesson for me to learn. "Do what you know to be right and everyone will like you" used to be my naïve belief. Now I know that if I do what I feel right about, all I have to worry about is God's approval. It's simpler that way and, furthermore, it works. In the Old Testament, when Noah stated his intention to build an ark, his friends scoffed at him. Yet he did not stop to deliberate or convince; he just went on building his ark. That is declaring.

In some ways, not only does declaring preserve our safety zones, but declaring itself becomes a safety zone. For it is a great relief to declare rather than to debate. Debating means that unless I can prove my point to someone else I cannot rest. Declaring, when it is based upon the safety zone of the will of God, does not mean that I just do my own thing regardless of right or wrong or the opinion of others. But it does mean that having once established what is right for me in a given situation, I can declare that position and rest in the knowledge of the will of God. I can say no to making cookies for the PTA, or serving on the pulpit committee, or driving children to summer camp, or even to answering a simple telephone call. I can say yes to a long, hot bath or even to a day spent doing nothing, if that is what I need.

Robert Louis Stevenson once wrote that "to be idle requires a strong sense of personal identity." And, indeed, to do nothing is for some of us a harder task than any other. Yet at times that is exactly what we need if we are to go on. Resting on the safety zone of the will of God, I can say no if I need to. And I can say yes also and feel good about myself regardless of human approval.

In the more complex and constantly fluctuating areas such as medical ethics, to declare means that I can decide upon a course of action and rest in that decision even though I may be in the middle of several conflicting opinions. In those areas where there are no established opinions, I can at least declare *for me*.

In his daily devotional book, *Morning and Evening,*
Charles Spurgeon said:

> Be assured that thy God will be thy counsellor and friend;
> He shall guide thee; He will direct all thy ways. In His
> written Word thou hast this assurance in part fulfilled, for
> holy Scripture is His counsel to thee. Happy are we to have
> God's Word always to guide us! What were the mariner
> without his compass? And what were the Christian without
> the Bible? This is the unerring chart, the map in which
> every shoal is described, and all the channels from the
> quicksands of destruction to the haven of salvation
> mapped and marked by One who knows all the way.[3]

The safety zone of the will of God and, then, the safety
zone of declaring—together they can transform chaos into
peace and productiveness.

It is only as we actively use and declare our safety zones
that we can then be equipped to grow. For without those
safety zones our lives will be too filled with frustration for
us to do much more than just survive. Safety zones make
growth possible. Yet growth involves change and newness;
and while growth challenges most of us it also scares us, for
it involves the unknown as opposed to the tried and true.
However, with a basis of good safety zones to buffer the
changes, growth becomes a realistic possibility. Only with
the support of those safety zones can we be willing to take
on the risk of growth.

It is impossible in the day in which we live for any of us to
say, as one woman did to me: "I will never change again!"
For in these times of rapid external change, not to change
is an impossibility. How we change, however, is very much
up to us. For while we may, at times, be totally unable to
control our circumstances, we can always choose our attitude toward those circumstances.

In some ways I believe that when that first atomic bomb
was dropped on Hiroshima, it became symbolic of the end
of a whole order of things and the start of a new world for

all of us. General Douglas MacArthur suggested this in his speech to the American people following the formal ceremonies of the surrender of Japan, which were held aboard the *USS Missouri* on 2 September 1945. He said,

> A new era is upon us. . . . The destructiveness of the war potential, through progressive advances in scientific discovery, has in fact now reached a point which revises the traditional concept of war. . . . We have had our last chance. If we do not now devise some greater and more equitable system, Armageddon will be at our door. The problem basically is theological and involves a spiritual recrudescence and improvement of human character that will synchronize with our almost matchless advances in science, art, literature, and all material and cultural developments of the past two thousand years. It must be of the spirit if we are to save the flesh.[3]

A new era is indeed upon us! Change is inevitable, for it is occurring all around us. We cannot choose to obliterate change. The choice which is ours, however, is whether to allow that change to affect our lives hit and miss without making our own personal choices—or to choose growth, to choose our attitude toward those changing circumstances. For the Christian, the idea of growth should not be such a new one, for Christ Himself came to this world to change people, not to leave them as they were. Change is a basic principle of Christian doctrine.

It is one of the miracles of nature that out of ugly cocoons, which would choke out life forever if they became permanent dwelling places, emerge some of the most beautiful creations of nature. Non-growth would stifle their very existence. Growth liberates their beauty as well as their full potential for life.

During a large part of my childhood, my family and I used to vacation in a little town in northern California, Carmel-by-the-Sea. We always stayed in a nearby town called Pacific Grove, where the magnificent monarch butterflies came every winter. It was a charming site: a log cabin in among huge trees, a lighthouse with a foghorn which had a tranquilizing effect on me as I fell asleep at night, the sea pounding on the rocky northern coast, and always the mysterious butterflies who came in the cold weather and left during the first warm days of spring.

As I grew older, I learned more about these butterflies who had so enchanted me in childhood. I discovered that the monarchs come each winter to Pacific Grove, where they live in a state of semi-hibernation, mainly resting while they stay alive by sipping nectar and water until spring. During that time their fat reserves build up and they gather strength for their long migration north. The trees of Pacific Grove are their safety zone. There they are refreshed and refurbished. Afterwards, it is in the north, where the milkweed plants grow, that they accomplish their life task of reproduction.

Once the egg is laid, the whole nine-month life cycle of the monarch butterfly alternates between safety zones and growth. The egg laid on the underside of a milkweed leaf from which the tiny caterpillar first emerges; the various outer skins of the growing caterpillar, shed four times in the course of its life; the chrysalis, hanging by a silk thread woven by the caterpillar, from which the final, adult monarch emerges—all of these provide protective chambers for the developing monarch in the same way that the trees growing in the fog by the sea offer shelter to the adult butterfly.

The safety zones are there for the developing monarch butterfly, but they are safety zones only if it leaves them! If it stays too long at any one of its stages of development, it will be smothered by its own safety zone and die. In its growth it struggles and fights to break the shell of the egg or to break out of its skins and its chrysalis each time it outgrows them. Then, finally, after its full development into a creature radiantly colored in orange, black, and white, the monarch butterfly migrates to its adult safety zone in the trees of Pacific Grove, where it rests and builds up for its return trip north.

In the reproductive process, as the caterpillar sheds one skin after another, it starts out whitish-gray in color and gradually adds its more distinctive shades of orange and black, thus more closely resembling the completed butterfly. As Christians, too, when we use our safety zones for growth, we struggle and change, and all the time we resemble more and more that finished product of being transformed into His image.

The Bible says, "But we all, with open face beholding as in a glass the glory of the Lord, are changed into the same image from glory to glory, even as by the Spirit of the Lord" (2 Cor. 3:18). Weymouth's translation of "from glory to glory" is "from one degree of radiant holiness to another."

The combination of growth, struggle and safety zones seems to make up a principle of living for all of God's creation. And the goal, whether it be physical or spiritual, is one of reproduction and growth.

We sometimes resist growth because it involves change and risk. Change involves new and untried territory, while risk involves potential gain but also potential loss. It is frightening to step out into that which is new, but to me it is even more frightening to step back into the dull flatness of what may seem like complete safety but in the end turns out to be spiritual and emotional death.

Once when I was very afraid of doing something which involved potential physical danger, I drove slowly by one of the most depressing convalescent homes I had ever visited and I made myself remember the living dead whom I had seen in that facility. The blank looks of some contrasted with the desperation in the eyes of others and their childlike pleas for help have haunted me ever since. These pathetic people were safe—fed, clothed, monitored, and locked up at night. But who would trade the life of highest risk for that kind of anesthetized safety? Who would choose to be one of those safe, miserable creatures—just to be safe?

Why grow? Because the opposite of growth is death on some level. It is impossible to just remain the same. Years ago, a poem from the works of Amy Carmichael influenced me deeply to go on. It still has the same effect on me:

> Make me Thy mountaineer;
> I would not linger on the lower slope.
> Fill me afresh with hope, O God of hope,
> That undefeated I may climb the hill
> As seeing Him who is invisible,
> Whom having not seen I love.
> O my Redeemer, when this little while
> Lies far behind me and the last defile
> Is all alight, and in that light I see
> My Saviour and my Lord, what will it be?[4]

I started to write this book just days after the death of my Aunt Lydia. Now it is almost summer, and I am nearing the end. This morning I had an insatiable longing to pull an old, metal covered, wooden table of hers out of storage to use in my kitchen, and so I did just that. My kitchen is really too small to contain it well, but as I stopped writing this afternoon and went out to the kitchen to look at what is now my table, I felt strangely comforted by its presence. I realized anew how effectively a small, valueless object can become a safety zone.

It's true that this particular table gives me the practical advantage of added baking space in a kitchen which is too small; yet underneath its wooden frame the paint is peeling and it certainly has little material value. And although a friend just came and said she thought it gave my kitchen a warm, homey look, but I'm not so sure she's not just being nice.

Still, for me that table is a safety zone of good memories of years past: drinking milk and eating cookies while I chatted in the kitchen with Aunt Lydia after school; watching my Aunt Ruth prepare dishes she had learned to cook when she was a missionary years ago in the north of China; joining my mother and my sister in my Aunt Lydia's kitchen while we "helped" with the finishing touches of Christmas Day dinner. Now, having that simple, unpretentious table makes me feel good all over again, and the positive tapes of the past begin to play.

It has not yet been quite a year since my Aunt Lydia's death marked the final loss of all of my relatives with whom I have any extensive relationship. But these months have been months of positive growth.

I miss my aunt, but I feel happy for her, too. For, in the words of Amy Carmichael once again, "what an awakening one who has walked with Him in the twilight must have, when suddenly she awakes in His likeness and the light is shining around her—all shadowy ways forgotten."[5] For Aunt Lydia, life was becoming shadowy. She was unable to take the walks of which she was so fond, or to read for any length of time because her eyesight was growing dim, or to remember with clarity the things she heard. Now the shadows are gone for her. That knowledge, too, is a safety zone for me.

The Lord indeed gave, and the Lord has taken away. In the meantime, for those of us who are left, "He setteth the solitary in families . . ." (Ps. 68:6), for He, more than anyone else, knows our need for safety zones if we are to fulfill His purpose for us on this earth.

For no matter how strong we may be, we are all vulnerable and fragile. A man lugged some furniture upstairs into his newly decorated apartment. Then, sitting on the stairs, he looked at me and said, "You know, I don't even know how to get my utilities turned on or how to wash my clothes. Sylvia always did that for me." Now, separated from his wife, Sylvia, this man had to face all the practical

157

details of his everyday living. Probably somewhere across town, Sylvia, too, was making adjustments, wondering what to do about the house insurance or how to fix the leaky faucet. Each were adults in their middle thirties. Each had gone straight from their parents' homes into this marriage some twelve years before. They had never really been on their own before. But now John, at least, felt something like a little boy—too old to cry and far from his boyhood safety zones where parents saw to his needs and tucked him safely into bed each night.

At times we all feel like little children again, vulnerable and alone. When my father died, I lost my father only. But when my mother died a few years later, I felt like I had lost both of my parents, including my father all over again. For the first time I realized, as Madeleine L'Engle had said, that I would never again be anyone's child. In a new way, I now felt thoroughly adult, even though I had been functioning as an adult for a long time. Yet I had my safety zones, too. One of them was my sense of meaning, for I had a commitment to my parents, to myself, and above all to God that I would go on, that I would grow.

As I was trying to recover myself on that weekend before my mother's funeral, I came across a tattered, framed copy of a poem by Robert Frost which, even though it was not new to me, somehow said it all in a way which I had never seen before. The poem became, for me, a safety zone of meaning, for it summarized both the refuge of safety zones and the eternal challenge to grow:

> Whose woods are these I think I know
> His house is in the village though;
> He will not see me stopping here
> To watch his woods fill up with snow.
>
> My little horse must think it queer
> To stop without a farmhouse near
> Between the woods and frozen lake
> The darkest evening of the year.

Miles to Go before I Sleep

He gives his harness bells a shake
To ask if there is some mistake.
The only other sound's the sweep
Of easy wind and downy flake.

The woods are lovely, dark and deep.
But I have promises to keep,
And miles to go before I sleep,
And miles to go before I sleep.[5]

Endnotes

Chapter 1

1. Joseph B. Fabry, *The Pursuit of Meaning* (New York: Harper & Row, 1980), 45.
2. Rollo May, *The Art of Counseling* (Nashville: Abingdon, 1967), 119.
3. Ibid., 162.
4. Amy Wilson Carmichael, "Rose from Friar," (London: SPCK, 1933), xxi.

Chapter 2

1. Vera Phillips and Edwin Robertson, *The Wounded Healer* (Grand Rapids, MI: Eerdmans, 1984), 79.
2. Ibid., 21.
3. Ibid., 25.
4. Joy Guinness, *Mrs. Howard Taylor, Her Web of Time* (London: Lutterworth Press, reprinted from original edition put out by China Inland Mission, 1952), 198–99.
5. Viktor E. Frankl, *The Will to Meaning* (New York: New American Library, 1969), 155–56.
6. William Shirer, *Twentieth Century Journey* (Boston: Little, Brown, 1976), 13–14.
7. Dr. and Mrs. Howard Taylor, *Hudson Taylor's Spiritual Secrets* (London/Philadelphia/Toronto/Melbourne/Shanghai: China Inland Mission, 1949), 86.
8. Ibid., 147.

Chapter 3

1. Paul Tournier, *A Place for You* (New York: Harper & Row, 1968), 9, 12.
2. Viktor E. Frankl, *The Doctor and the Soul* (New York: Vintage, 1973), 44.
3. Ibid., 46.
4. Frank Clifford, "Protest Has No Effect on Abortions," *Los Angeles Times*, 23 January 1983, Part I, p. 3.

5. Betty Friedan, "The Value of Love," (interview with Sherrye Henry) *Vogue,* March 1982.

6. Walter Lippman, quoted in Joseph B. Fabry, *The Pursuit of Meaning* (Boston: Beacon, 1968), 101.

Chapter 4

1. Madeleine L'Engle, *The Irrational Season* (New York: Seabury, 1979), 46–47.

2. Viktor E. Frankl, *The Will to Meaning* (New York: New American Library, 1969), 132.

3. Amy Carmichael, *Whispers of His Power* (Old Tappan, New Jersey: Revell, 1982), 83.

Chapter 5

1. Elizabeth Sherrill, "Hallelujah, Hallelujah, Hallelujah!" *Guideposts,* December 1985, 30.

2. "Only the Best," *Los Angeles Times Magazine,* 15 December 1985, excerpted from Stuart E. Jacobson and Jill Spalding, *Only the Best: A Celebration of Gift Giving in America* (New York: Abrams, 1985), 18.

3. "Rabbi Ben Ezra," in *Poems of Robert Browning,* ed. Donald Smalley (Boston: Houghton Mifflin, 1956), 287.

4. Ibid., 282.

5. Hudson Taylor, *To China with Love* (Minneapolis: Bethany, 1972), 9.

Chapter 6

1. A. A. Milne, *The World of Pooh* (New York: Dutton, 1957), 45–46.

2. Catherine Marshall, *Beyond Ourselves* (New York: Avon, 1961), 154.

3. Agatha Christie, "Go Back for Murder" in *The Mousetrap & Other Plays* (New York: Bantam, 1981), 696.

Chapter 7

1. Sid Huff with Joe Alex Morris, *My Fifteen Years with General MacArthur* (New York: Paperback Library, Inc., 1964), 120.

2. W. H. Thompson, "Assignment: Churchill", *Reader's Digest,* March 1955, 161–62.

3. Walter Laquer, *The Terrible Secret* (Boston, Toronto: Little, Brown and Company, 1980), 1.

4. Dr. Rollo May, *Man's Search for Himself* (New York: W. W. Norton & Company, Inc., 1953), 100.

5. Ibid., 99.

Chapter 8

1. Helmut Thielicke, *Encounter with Spurgeon,* trans. by John W. Doberstein (Grand Rapids: Baker Book House, © 1963 by Fortress Press, 1975), 11.

Endnotes

2. Charles H. Spurgeon, *Morning & Evening: Daily Readings* (Grand Rapids: Zondervan Publishing House, 1963), 490.

3. General Douglas MacArthur, *Reminiscences* (New York: Time, Inc., 1964), 276.

4. Amy Carmichael, *Gold by Moonlight* (Fort Washington, PA: Christian Literature Crusade, 1970), 75.

5. Amy Carmichael, *Candles in the Dark* (Fort Washington, PA: Christian Literature Crusade, 1982), 59.

6. Robert Frost, "Stopping by Woods on a Snowy Evening" (New Hampshire: Holt, Rinehart & Winston, 1923). From *The Poetry of Robert Frost* edited by Edward Connery Lathem. Copyright 1923, © 1969 by Holt, Rinehart and Winston. Copyright 1951 by Robert Frost. Reprinted by permission of Henry Holt and Company.